C000023568

Opening up
Ezekiel's visions

PETER JEFFERY

DayOne

'Ezekiel, a much neglected Old Testament prophet, speaks across the centuries in this straightforward and down-to-earth explanation of his message. Clearly written, with no punches pulled as far as contemporary application is concerned, this is just the sort of help needed by those who otherwise might find the book difficult to understand. Once again Peter Jeffery has succeeded in bringing home to twenty-first century people God's ever relevant diagnosis of their condition and his remedy for it.'

Graham Harrison, MA, B.Litt.,
Minister of Emmanuel Chapel, Newport and Lecturer in Christian Doctrine, London Theological Seminary

'Peter Jeffery is a crystal-clear communicator. You could not miss his point if you tried. Being called to feed God's sheep, he does it better than most. Some men can feed giraffes, those tall, ungainly intellectuals who nibble at the tops of the trees. But how many can truly be said to feed the sheep? How often do ordinary people feel that what they heard was too intellectual and not applicable where they live and work, play and die? Peter is one of the best at bringing the truth of God's Word to the level where we can reach it. See if Ezekiel does not open up for you under Peter's warm teaching. See if you are not challenged with the reality of God himself. Peter writes to help, to warn, to turn on lights, to apply salve, to comfort, to show you the glory of God in the face of Jesus Christ. I only wish I had Peter's help on my first trip through Ezekiel's visions years ago.'

Steve Martin,
Pastor, Heritage Church, Fayetteville,GA., Chairman of Missions Committee, ARBCA

© Day One Publications 2004

First printed 2004

Scripture quotations are from the NIV, International Bible Society,
1984

ISBN 1 903087 66-X

British Library Cataloguing in Publication Data available

Published by Day One Publications

Ryelands Road, Leominster, HR6 8NZ

Telephone 01568 613 740   FAX 01568 611 473

email—sales@dayone.co.uk

web site—www.dayone.co.uk

Designed by Steve Devane and printed by Gutenberg Press, Malta

6

OPENING UP EZEKIEL'S VISIONS

List of Bible abbreviations

THE OLD TESTAMENT		1 Chr.	1 Chronicles	Dan.	Daniel
		2 Chr.	2 Chronicles	Hosea	Hosea
Gen.	Genesis	Ezra	Ezra	Joel	Joel
Exod.	Exodus	Neh.	Nehemiah	Amos	Amos
Lev.	Leviticus	Esth.	Esther	Obad.	Obadiah
Num.	Numbers	Job	Job	Jonah	Jonah
Deut.	Deuteronomy	Ps.	Psalms	Micah	Micah
Josh.	Joshua	Prov.	Proverbs	Nahum	Nahum
Judg.	Judges	Eccles.	Ecclesiastes	Hab.	Habakkuk
Ruth	Ruth	S.of.S.	Song of Solomon	Zeph.	Zephaniah
1 Sam.	1 Samuel	Isa.	Isaiah	Hag.	Haggai
2 Sam.	2 Samuel	Jer.	Jeremiah	Zech.	Zechariah
1 Kings	1 Kings	Lam.	Lamentations	Mal.	Malachi
2 Kings	2 Kings	Ezek.	Ezekiel		

THE NEW TESTAMENT		Gal.	Galatians	Heb.	Hebrews
		Eph.	Ephesians	James	James
Matt.	Matthew	Phil.	Philippians	1 Peter	1 Peter
Mark	Mark	Col.	Colossians	2 Peter	2 Peter
Luke	Luke	1 Thes.	1 Thessalonians	1 John	1 John
John	John	2 Thes.	2 Thessalonians	2 John	2 John
Acts	Acts	1 Tim.	1 Timothy	3 John	3 John
Rom.	Romans	2 Tim.	2 Timothy	Jude	Jude
1 Cor.	1 Corinthians	Titus	Titus	Rev.	Revelation
2 Cor.	2 Corinthians	Philem.	Philemon		

Overview and Structure

Ezekiel lived about six hundred years before the time of Christ and his ministry took place during a time of important transition in the life of the nation of Israel—a time when the judgement of God would bring catastrophic change to the lives of its people. During Ezekiel's ministry, such things as the following would take place:

• Jerusalem would come under siege and be destroyed;

• The temple would be burnt;

• The monarchy would come to an end;

• Much of the population of Judah would be taken as captives into exile in Babylon.

At this time, balances in power were shifting. To the south, Egypt, once a superpower, was in decline, and Assyria's influence from the north, too, was becoming less and less significant. However, Babylon (in modern-day Iraq) was becoming extremely strong. In approximately 601-600 B.C., one of the last kings of Judah, Jehoakim, tried to rebel against the overshadowing power of Babylon—but, to no avail. The result was a siege of Jerusalem by Nebuchadnezzar in 597 B.C. Some ten thousand of its people were taken into captivity in Babylon (see 2 Kings 24:14), and Ezekiel was among them.

Although Ezekiel was a priest (see Ezek. 1:3), God called him to be a prophet, too, and he came to be highly regarded as such—even though his words were not always taken to heart by his hearers. Many of his prophecies were accompanied by symbolic actions (or 'visual aids' as they have also been described).

Ezekiel's prophetic ministry lasted over twenty years (from 593-571 B.C.). Chapters 1-32 are largely warnings of disaster, whereas chapters 33-49 are, more positively, promises of hope. The fall of Jerusalem (Ezek. 33:21-22) is the turning point of the book.

TIMELINE SHOWING THE CONTE

ISRAEL UNDER
THE JUDGES

ISRAEL AS A
UNITED KINGDOM

ISRAEL
DIVIDED

NORTHERN
KINGDOM

SOUTHERN
KINGDOM

ISAIAH

F THE MINISTRY OF EZEKIEL

| SUPERPOWER: BABYLON | SUPERPOWER: PERSIA | SUPERPOWER: GREECE | SUPERPOWER: ROME |

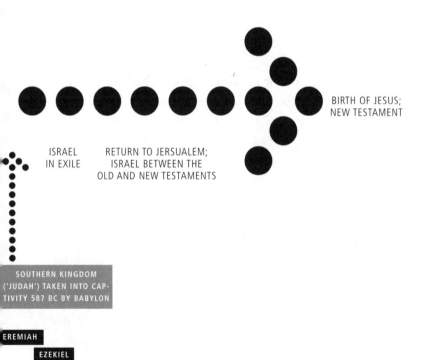

BIRTH OF JESUS; NEW TESTAMENT

ISRAEL IN EXILE

RETURN TO JERSUALEM; ISRAEL BETWEEN THE OLD AND NEW TESTAMENTS

SOUTHERN KINGDOM ('JUDAH') TAKEN INTO CAPTIVITY 587 BC BY BABYLON

EREMIAH

EZEKIEL

DANIEL

OPENING UP EZEKIEL'S VISIONS

1 Who was Ezekiel?

This book is not a commentary on the book of Ezekiel, but, as the title suggests, it is a series of lessons and principles derived from some of Ezekiel's visions. We shall seek to draw out lessons applicable to today's Christians from this remarkable Old Testament book, but first of all we have to see who Ezekiel was.

For some time the people of God had been divided, with the ten tribes known as Israel in the north, and the other two tribes of Judah in the south—see the timeline on page 10. King Solomon died in 931 B.C. and was succeeded by his son Rehoboam. This foolish man alienated the already disgruntled northern tribes (1 Kings 12), and, as a result, his kingdom collapsed. As the king of Judah, he continued to rule from Jerusalem over two tribes (Judah and Benjamin), while Jeroboam ruled as the king of Israel in the north over the other ten tribes. Thus the people of God were divided and at war with one another. This tragic situation continued for 350 years until God finally brought the whole sad story to an end. In 586 B.C., he allowed Nebuchadnezzar, king of Babylon, to destroy the Southern Kingdom. The Northern Kingdom had already fallen to

Assyria in 722 B.C., so now both kingdoms had come to an end and very many of the people were in exile in foreign lands.

Jeremiah had prophesied that the Babylonian exile would last for seventy years (Jer. 25:11). This was God's judgement upon them—but it was more than that, for, during the exile, God was going to refine these people in the crucible of suffering. His purpose was to create in them a new heart, so that he could bring them back to their own land to serve him as they ought (Jer. 24:5-7). The prophet Ezekiel was raised up by God to minister to the people during the Babylonian exile.

R.C. Sproul and Robert Wolgemuth have written:

The time between the fall of Israel and the demise of Judah was one of unmatched turbulence in the Southern Kingdom. It was during this time that Hezekiah reigned as king. He was a good king, a godly king. It was his desire to restore Judah to obedience and proper worship. But Hezekiah's reign and God's blessing on Jerusalem lasted only a few years. His son, Manasseh, a very wicked king, replaced the righteous and God-fearing Hezekiah. Not only did Manasseh establish pagan images in the hilltop sites—high places—around Jerusalem, he also brought a pagan image into the very temple of God. Incredibly, and by God's grace, Manasseh repented as an old man. His successor, unfortunately, was his nefarious son, who had learnt by his father's early example. Until Josiah came to power, Judah found itself in an ongoing and terrible descent.[1]

Josiah's reforms held back the judgement of God upon Judah for a while but inevitably the Babylonians invaded and the Babylonian captivity began.

Ezekiel—his name means 'God strengthens'—was a priest who had been taken into exile with the rest of Judah. It was in Babylon that he was set apart by God to be a prophet (Ezek. 2:5). His whole ministry was in Babylon to a people under judgement and his message was of more judgement to come, but also of restoration and blessing from God. The judgement in some cases was terrible. To quote Sproul and Wolgemuth again:

> In fact, God's ultimate punishment is not when he disciplines, but when he walks away. His final act of reproof is when he allows his children to live unfettered and undisciplined lives without his chastening.[2]

Ezekiel used amazing word pictures to communicate his message. These visions of God convey a message that is as relevant today as it was 2,500 years ago when Ezekiel first spoke them.

> Ezekiel's name was very symbolic, meaning 'God strengthens'.

FOR FURTHER STUDY

1. Read Ezek. 1:1-2, 28b and note the various ways in which these verses suggest how God-centred Ezekiel's ministry was going to be, and yet how closely he was associated with the people he ministered to.

2. Read Ezek. 2:1-7. Mention at least one other Old Testament prophet who was called to a similarly difficult ministry.

TO THINK ABOUT AND DISCUSS

1. God often warns before he sends final judgement upon people. How do you think Ezekiel's ministry demonstrates this principle?

2. Ezek. 2:7 emphasizes that the prophet must speak 'my' (God's) words to the people. Suggest how this shows that some modern ministers are guilty of misleading their congregations when they bring another message, one that is at odds with the revealed truth of God in the Bible.

2 Lessons not learnt

Ezekiel Chapter 8

As the Lord took hold of Ezekiel and showed him unusual and symbolic visions, it was his responsibility to relay God's word to the people to whom he ministered—and this was surely no easy task!

The people of Judah had seen how God dealt with Israel in 722 B.C. They knew that was the judgement of God and that they were not a lot better than Israel, so there was a strong possibility that they, too, could end up in captivity. The sin of Israel that led to God allowing Assyria to invade their land is summarized in 2 Kings 17:7-12. Judah was not innocent in this, and so 'the LORD warned Israel and Judah through all his prophets and seers ... but they would not listen and were as stiff-necked as their fathers, who did not trust in the LORD their God.' (vv. 13, 14).

God rejected both Israel and Judah but Assyria attacked only Israel at this time. Perhaps the people of Judah thought they had escaped divine wrath, and maybe they convinced themselves that they were not as bad as their northern cousins were. Whatever their thinking, there was little change in their attitude towards God. Idolatry continued but still God's hand of judgement was spared them. It seemed that they were getting away with their sin!

Unfortunately for man, no sin is ever left undealt with by God. The judgement may be delayed but it will most certainly come. One of the great fallacies of men and women is to assume that God does not care. The longer people go on in their sin, the more bold and arrogant they become in their defiance of God. Jeremiah, describing the people of his day, said that 'they have no shame at all, they do not even know how to blush.' (Jer. 6:15).

Today's society is very much like the one Jeremiah described. Sin is so blatant that, rather than blush at it, people delight in it. Sin has become the centre of entertainment—it is applauded but never repented of. Indeed, with this arrogance of sin, the word 'repentance' has all but vanished from the religious vocabulary. Even a system of religious evangelicalism has been concocted that makes repentance unnecessary. Today, it seems, a person can be saved without a conviction of the sin he or she needs to be saved from.

Like Judah, we never learn. The past is forgotten as if there are no lessons to be learnt. Judah saw all that had happened to Israel but assumed it could never happen to them. But it did!

Judah invaded

Eventually Assyria turned its attention to Judah, and Sennacherib invaded the land during the reign of Hezekiah. Hezekiah was a good man and had instigated reforms in Judah (2 Chr. 31:20-21). At first he was afraid and prepared to negotiate with the Assyrians (2 Kings 18:13-16). But you can never satisfy the demands of the enemies of God. The king of Judah was to learn that his only hope was in the Lord, and he turned to God in prayer (2 Kings 19:14-19). The result was that the ambitions of Assyria were destroyed by the power of God (2 Kings 19:35-37).

How deep the conviction was in the hearts of the people concerning the reform of Hezekiah is doubtful because, soon after his days, they turned back enthusiastically to idols. The fifty-five year reign of Manasseh, Hezekiah's son, must have deeply grieved the heart of God (2 Chr. 33:1-9). Judah was now guilty of doing more evil even than the Assyrians. For a while there were more reforms under Josiah but the heart of Judah was set to disobey the Lord until inevitably God sent Nebuchadnezzar, the king of Babylon, to deal with them.

In all God's mercy and dealings with them, Judah had learnt nothing. We read that 'the LORD, the God of their fathers, sent word to them through his messengers again and again, because he had pity on his people and on his dwelling place. But they mocked God's messengers, despised his words and scoffed at his prophets until the wrath of the LORD was aroused against his people and there was no remedy' (2 Chr. 36:15-16). There was left to God no remedy of grace—only the remedy of judgement.

Babylon

It might be thought that Babylon would sober the thinking of Judah, and for some, indeed, it did. Psalm 137 records the lament of a people in judgement: 'By the rivers of Babylon we sat and wept when we remembered Zion… How can we sing the songs of the LORD while in a foreign land?' (vv. 1, 4). All this is commendable but it does not appear to be the general attitude of the people. When God called Ezekiel to be a prophet, he warned him the task would not be easy because Judah was still 'a rebellious nation that has rebelled against me; they and their fathers have been in revolt against me to this very day. The people to whom I am sending you are obstinate and stubborn.' (Ezek. 2:3, 4).

The words 'to this very day' reveal a people who had learnt nothing over the past sorry years. They were as rebellious to God in Babylon as they had been in Judah. So the first part of Ezekiel's book is a pronouncement of judgement. In their obstinacy, they took God for granted; and in their spiritual blindness, they committed over and over again the worst possible sin of idolatry.

> In their obstinacy, they took God for granted; and in their spiritual blindness, they committed over and over again the worst possible sin of idolatry.

In chapter 8:12-16, God showed Ezekiel this sin of idolatry and these verses show us why idolatry is so evil. It is a corruption of true worship and it robs God of his glory as nothing else can. It puts in God's place a dull, lifeless object.

Matthew Henry has said of Ezekiel 8:14:

> An abominable thing indeed, that they should choose rather
> to serve an idol in tears than to serve the true God with
> joyfulness and gladness of heart! Yet such absurdities as these
> are those guilty of who follow after lying vanities and forsake
> their own mercies... These mourning women sat at the door
> of the gate of the Lord's house, and there shed their
> idolatrous tears, as it were in defiance of God and the sacred
> rites of his worship.[3]

The reason the people behaved like this is given in verse
12—'They say, "The LORD does not see us; the LORD has
forsaken the land."'

The all-seeing God

My three-year-old granddaughter was visiting us one
summer's day and we were out in the garden. She wanted to
do something that I had told her she should not do. So she
said to me, 'Grandpa, close your eyes.' Her idea was that if
my eyes were closed, I would not be able to see her and she
could do the thing I had told her not to do. Such thinking may
be cute in a three-year-old, but it is disastrous in adults,
especially when they think God does not see them. Such
thinking is sheer stupidity, as Psalm 44:20-21 makes clear: 'If
we had forgotten the name of our God or spread out our
hands to a foreign god, would not God have discovered it,
since he knows the secrets of the heart?'

Judah said the Lord had forsaken the land because they were not in the Promised Land but instead in a foreign land. Consider again the words of Matthew Henry:

> This was a blasphemous reflection upon God, as if he had forsaken them first, else they would not have forsaken him. Note, those are ripe indeed for ruin who have arrived at such a pitch of impudence as to lay the blame of their sins upon God himself.[4]

Clearly, there was no sense of guilt and no spirit of repentance in these people.

All this took place some 2,500 years ago, but it is still very relevant to us today. People say, 'God is dead so we can forget him and do as we please. He can't see us, and, even if he could, he would not care. If you want to worship some celebrity or sports or pop idol, that is all right. God is dead.' You only have to see how those who hate God prosper to prove that. The wicked prosper and sin is not punished. Our nations have legalized homosexuality and abortion, so, they argue, 'Let's now legalize euthanasia and let's allow local councils to run brothels. We must be up-to-date. God does not care.'

However, God does care. He is always God and he will never ignore our sinful acts. He said of Judah, 'I will deal with them in anger' (Ezek. 8:18). There are times in Scripture when God deals with our sin in love, but Ezekiel

> God does care. He is always God and he will never ignore our sinful acts.

reminds us that we are not to presume on divine love because God also deals with sin in anger. That is why he has prepared a hell as well as a heaven. People today choose to ignore this; they preach no judgement and no hell; they learn nothing from what the Lord has said and done. Such spiritual blindness is frightening indeed.

FOR FURTHER STUDY

1. Compare the list of detestable things mentioned in Ezek. 8 with the Ten Commandments (Exod. 20:1-17, Deut. 5:1-22).

2. When the temple at Jerusalem was first consecrated, there was a great display of the glory and power of the Lord. This was at first so great that even the priests could not perform their service (2 Chr. 5:14). How could it be that worship and activity in the temple had become so corrupt that the situation had reached the extreme degree recorded in Ezekiel's vision?

TO THINK ABOUT AND DISCUSS

1. As the Southern Kingdom of Judah progressed in sin and ungodliness, the Lord sent prophets to warn them to repent. What parallels do you see between this and your own nation?

2. It has been said that the modern church is 'soft on sin'. Do you agree with such a statement? Suggest examples from real life to substantiate your viewpoint.

3. Mention as many examples as possible of the grace and patience of God to be seen in your own society today.

4. Look up Rom. 2:4 in context and note how God's kindness is intended not to excuse people in their sins, but to lead them out of their sins. How does knowing this help you to approach people with the message of the gospel?

3 Sweet words of truth

Ezekiel Chapters 2 and 3

The people of Judah had learnt nothing from seeing God's dealings with Israel, nor from their own captivity in Babylon, so would they learn anything from Ezekiel? Would a people who were obstinate and stubborn even listen to a prophet? These things may well have gone through Ezekiel's mind as he contemplated God's call to him to minister to Judah.

T he Lord anticipated this and told Ezekiel not to be concerned with their response—'whether they listen or fail to listen' (Ezek. 2:5), he had to bring them God's word. This does not mean that God was indifferent to their response; indeed, he longed that they should hear his word and believe. He was to plead with them, 'Rid yourselves of all the offences you have committed, and get a new heart and a new spirit. Why will you die, O house of Israel? For I take no pleasure in the death of anyone, declares the Sovereign LORD. Repent and live!' (Ezek. 18:31-32).

The very fact that God sent Ezekiel to them during their time under judgement in Babylon was an indication of how much he loved them. The initial purpose of Ezekiel's preaching was that they should know 'that a prophet has been among them.' (Ezek. 2:5). Whether they believed or not, they were being shown that God was still speaking to them. If there was a prophet among them, it was because God had sent him. So even Ezekiel's presence was proof of divine concern for their condition.

Hope

There are few things more revealing about the character of God than that he keeps sending preachers to bring his Word, even though people will not listen. There is always hope when God's Word is preached, and a nation can never know a more terrible situation than to have a famine of God's Word. In Wales, where I live, there is probably more faithful biblical preaching today than there has been for a hundred years. Yet sadly the Word is falling on deaf ears and there are very few conversions taking place. In fact, there are few who even hear it because few attend church on Sundays. But still the Word is there; God, in his mercy, still sends preachers. They may not be valued or appreciated but their presence is a token of hope.

If the Lord were to shut this door and remove his servants, what would happen? Faith comes through hearing God's Word (Rom. 10:17) so, if no gospel is preached, there can be no faith and there can be no hope. There is no greater darkness than the darkness of no gospel. It is a darkness so intense that nothing challenges sin, nothing addresses itself to the sinner's conscience and nothing can provoke the sinner to seek a better way. The darkness of a people who hear God's Word and then reject it is nothing like as terrible as the darkness of a people who never hear what the Lord has to say.

At the beginning of the twenty-first century, Britain is a place of great spiritual ignorance. Generations have grown up who have never been to Sunday school or church and who know nothing of the mercies of God. If they think of God at all, it is with blurred and distorted concepts. We are like Judah in Babylon—obstinate, stubborn and rebellious—but still God allows his Word to come to this nation. When the Word is preached, there is always hope and anything can happen.

> There is no greater darkness than the darkness of no gospel.

Ignorance

If the preaching of the Word offers hope to sinners, it also takes away all excuse for sin. Whether they listen or fail to listen, people are confronted with the truth, and the same truth that can save will also condemn. People have a self-imposed ignorance. Paul deals with the question of ignorance in Romans 10.

The Israelites were not atheists or agnostics but people who were zealous for God. Their problem was ignorance. Their zeal was not based on knowledge. The sort of knowledge to which Paul refers has nothing to do with a person's intellectual ability, but is a knowledge that even a child can possess. Neither was their ignorance the result of the truth being hidden from them. They were ignorant in the presence of knowledge. The last verse of Romans 10 is a quotation from Isaiah 65:2: 'All day long I have held out my hands to a disobedient and obstinate people.' If you look up that verse in Isaiah, you will see that it goes on to say, '…people, who walk in ways not good, pursuing their own imaginations.'

It does not matter where a person begins the journey of faith—whether as an atheist, agnostic, or a deeply religious man or woman. What is common to all people when they think about God is what Paul calls 'zeal … not based on knowledge', and what Isaiah describes as 'pursuing their own imaginations'. The atheist says, 'There is no God.' The agnostic says, 'It is not possible to know.' The religious person says, 'There is a God and this is how I perceive him to be.' Basically there is little or no difference in any of these three responses. All three are people making pronouncements about God.

The Bible message tells us, in effect, to stop talking, to be quiet and listen to what God has to say: 'Faith comes from hearing the message, and the message is heard through the word of Christ' (Rom. 10:17). The Israelites, though deeply religious, were not listening to God. Because of this, they did not know the true message of the gospel and had concocted a way of salvation which was unacceptable to God. This compulsive tendency in people of producing a do-it-yourself way of salvation is one of the major obstacles to a true faith in God. Wherever it is present, there will inevitably be a rejection of God's way of salvation.

The Scroll

> Clearly, it was no pleasant message Ezekiel was to deliver ...

It was not a very hopeful prospect that was set before Ezekiel, but it was one he could not avoid without being as rebellious as the people he was to preach to (Ezek. 2:8). God encouraged him by showing him a scroll on which 'were written words of lament and mourning and woe'. (Ezek. 2:10). Clearly, it was no pleasant message Ezekiel was to deliver and this must have further discouraged him. Then he was given the strange command to eat the scroll! Before it was delivered to a sinful people, the message was to be devoured by the prophet.

He obeyed, probably with a measure of trepidation, but to his surprise the scroll 'tasted as sweet as honey in my mouth' (Ezek. 3:3). R. C. Sproul has commented:

> Imagine the consequences of all the sins of all God's chosen people being recorded on a scroll—Ezekiel called them lamentations, mourning, and woe. What a horrible document that must have been. Then God tells Ezekiel to eat the scroll, to literally ingest it, paper and all—enough to make a man sick. With this vision, you would think that God was telling Ezekiel that the sins of the Israelites were enough to make him nauseated. But there is a wonderful twist to the vision. The scroll tasted like honey. Not only did it not sicken the prophet, it was pleasing to his palate. As a priest, it was Ezekiel's job to plead the people's case before the righteous Judge, to bring their sins before him. And now he was

experiencing in a palpable way, the assurance—and the sweetness—of God's ultimate grace extended to the children of Israel.[5]

There is a sweetness in the truth of God even when it denounces our sin. The law is as much from God as is the grace of the gospel, and without the law we will never see our need of grace. One of the basic problems with man is that he does not take sin seriously and this is because he does not take God seriously. There is always the tendency to reduce God to manageable terms. Every system of religion, apart from biblical Christianity, does this. A. W. Tozer wrote:

> Among the sins to which the human heart is prone hardly any other is more hateful to God than idolatry, for idolatry is at bottom a libel on his character. The idolatrous heart assumes that God is other than he is—in itself a monstrous sin—and substitutes for the true God one made after his own likeness. Always this god will conform to the image of the one who created it and it will be base or pure, cruel or kind, according to the moral state of the mind from which it emerges.[6]

It is this thinking that lies behind the saying: 'The God I believe in would never send people to hell.' The only answer to such an unbiblical idea is to see and appreciate God as the Holy One. As we understand more of God's holiness, we shall also inevitably

> There is a sweetness in the truth of God even when it denounces our sin.

understand more of human sinfulness and the necessity of Christ's atoning death. God's holiness is revealed gloriously in the law and the cross.

God is holy and everything he does and instigates is holy. This is seen clearly in the law; its commandments are 'holy, righteous and good'. (Rom. 7:12). The law forbids sin in all its forms because sin is repugnant to God's holiness and pollutes and harms his creation. If the law cannot restrict sin, then God will destroy sin. God's wrath and justice are direct consequences of his holiness. God hates sin, just as a mother hates a disease that is killing her child. The law pushes the sinner into a corner and kicks away the crutches he or she has been depending upon—and so the sinner feels useless and hopeless. But this is the point at which we must arrive if we are to embrace by faith what Christ has done to redeem lost sinners such as we are. As C.H. Spurgeon once said, 'A man is never so near grace as when he begins to feel he can do nothing at all.'

> God hates sin, just as a mother hates a disease that is killing her child.

The law of God is as sweet as the gospel because it works with the grace of God to bring a sinner to salvation. Ezekiel had a hard message to deliver and there would be no hope for these obstinate, stubborn, rebellious people unless they heard it. If he had any reluctance to preach God's word to his people, the episode of the scroll removed it. Dennis Lane has written:

> Ezekiel was now beginning to see more clearly the role he was to play. His vision of God had an end in view, and that end was

a message from God to his own contemporaries, which they had no inclination to accept but which they needed to hear. Equipped to understand their opposition, Ezekiel found to his surprise that accepting God's purpose for himself and his people was finally sweet to his taste. The vision renewed his conviction and experience, and the word imparted content and direction. He could not have managed without either. Nor could he have survived without God's enabling power day by day.[7]

For further study ▶

FOR FURTHER STUDY

1. Look up the following references and suggest what is common to them all: Jer. 15:16; Rev. 10:9-10; Job 23:12.

2. Read Ezek. 3:7-9 and note the stubbornness of the people. Compare these verses with the following passages: 1 Sam. 8:7; Ps. 32:8, 9.

TO THINK ABOUT AND DISCUSS

1. If people's lives are to be transformed, it is vital that they be exposed to the Word of God, yet often in the church today the focus of activity is away from studying the Scriptures and Bible-based sermons. List some activities you know of which could be given more biblical content or substituted with more Bible-based activities.

2. What are some of the hindrances that may prevent the Scriptures from being opened more consistently and regularly in your church or fellowship group? What practical steps could you take to help correct this situation?

4 Grace in judgement

Ezekiel Chapter 9

Arthur Pink once very graphically described our sins as 'high provocations against the very gates of heaven.' Indeed, all sin invites the swift judgement of our holy God. And yet, in wrath, God does remember mercy (Hab. 3:2).

In chapter 9, Ezekiel sees a vision of judgement. Six men, angels, each with a deadly weapon, are sent by God to Jerusalem. Earlier in history, God had sent two angels to destroy Sodom and Gomorrah (Gen. 19:1-29), but here there are six. God is not here dealing with ignorant pagans but with his own people who have rejected his truth and light. He deals with them with an anger that seems to allow for no mercy. God says, 'I will not look on them with pity or spare them. Although they shout in my ears, I will not listen to them.' (Ezek. 8:18).

The instructions given to these six in verses 5 and 6 are frightening. No pity or mercy is to be shown and there are to be no exceptions. Even religion will not deliver them, because the judgement is to start at God's sanctuary. The temptation for many people may be to say how cruel all this was, and to reinforce their opinion that the God of the Old Testament was a harsh, vindictive God, unlike the God of the New Testament. However, a more balanced and sensible response to this judgement is to say how holy and righteous the Lord is. Everything here is in line with what the New Testament teaches about God. God is always holy as well as loving, and both law and grace reflect the true character of the Lord.

Warning

Do we think that God is indifferent to the godlessness and immorality of today? Do we believe that God has become all modern and progressive and changed his pronouncements upon sin? Do we think that hell-fire is rather old fashioned in the twenty-first century? If we do, it is only because we will not take God and sin seriously. Nothing happens in judgement that God has not warned about a hundred times before. The wage of sin has always been death.

In Genesis 6, man's sin caused the holy God to be sorry that he ever made men and women, and his verdict was that enough was enough: 'My spirit will not contend with man for ever, for he is mortal; his days will be a hundred and twenty years.' (Gen. 6:3). The judgement that the Lord pronounces in verse 7—'I will wipe mankind, whom I have created, from the face of the earth'—is devastating. Yet it is perfectly just! The terms of man's existence on earth had been violated, and the God who created man was also able to remove him from the earth. Note that even in this exercise of legitimate justice, God still offers man mercy and gives him a hundred and twenty years to consider his ways and repent. God always goes beyond what we might expect and he fixes one last period for the repentance of mankind. But would that period of a hundred and twenty years make any difference? We can see, now, that it did not, but the glory of grace is in the Lord who offers it, not in the sinner who may or may not receive it. God introduced into that one hundred and twenty year period a factor that grace always delights in: Noah began to undertake a ministry to his contemporaries. He was, says the apostle Peter, a preacher of righteousness (2 Peter 2:5).

Mercy

God is slow to anger, and even in this awful scene in Ezekiel 9 we can see the love and mercy of God shining brightly. We can see a man clothed in linen. Who is this man? If you compare Daniel 10:5-6 with Revelation 1:13-15, you can see that he is none other than the Lord Jesus Christ.

> I looked up and there before me was a man dressed in linen, with a belt of the finest gold round his waist. His body was like chrysolite, his face like lightning, his eyes like flaming torches, his arms and legs like the gleam of burnished bronze, and his voice like the sound of a multitude
> (Dan. 10:5-6).

> And among the lampstands was someone 'like a son of man,' dressed in a robe reaching down to his feet and with a golden

sash around his chest. His head and hair were white like wool, as white as snow, and his eyes were like blazing fire. His feet were like bronze glowing in a furnace, and his voice was like the sound of rushing waters
(Rev. 1:13-15).

Matthew Henry has written:

Here the honours of the pen exceeded those of the sword, but he was the Lord of angels that made use of the writer's inkhorn; for it is generally agreed, among the best interpreters that this man represented Christ as Mediator saving those that are his from the flaming sword of divine justice, he is our high priest, clothed with holiness, for that was signified by fine linen (Rev. 19:18). As a prophet he wears the writer's inkhorn... It is a matter of great comfort to all good Christians that, in the midst of the destroyers and the destructions that are abroad, there is a Mediator, a great high priest, who has an interest in heaven, and whom saints on earth have an interest in.[8]

In the Old Testament there are phenomena that have been called *theophanies*. These are visual manifestations of the presence of the Son of God. They are not incarnations of Jesus but temporary appearances of Jesus to meet particular needs. This is what we have in Ezekiel 9.

Before judgement falls, God sends Jesus with a pen and inkpot. His instructions are clear, to 'put a mark on the foreheads of those who grieve and lament over all the detestable things that are done' (Ezek. 9:4). So there were at least some who were not idolaters, but why were they different? They grieved over sin not because they were not sinners themselves, but because they knew they were sinners! They were aware of the pull of sin in their hearts and temptation was real to them. They knew what it was to fail, and they grieved over their own sin. The difference between them and the rest of the people was that they did not say, 'The LORD does not see us,'—they knew he did. They took their sin seriously because they knew that the Lord had not forsaken the earth. So they cried to God for mercy and pardon both for themselves and others. There was that essential quality with them that God demands when repentance takes place.

> They knew what it was to fail, and they grieved over their own sin.

God sent Jesus to these people to mark them on the forehead. The term 'forehead' tells us two things—the mark is on individuals, and it is very prominent. Matthew Henry made the point that the mark was

> to signify that God owns them for his own, and he will confess them another day. A work of grace in the soul is to God a mark on the forehead, which he will acknowledge as his mark, and by which he knows those that are his.[9]

The picture in Ezekiel 9 is of Jesus at work with pen and ink. But it is only a picture; the true mark of grace is not made with ink, but with the blood of Christ. The purpose of the mark was to distinguish, in a time of judgement, God's people from the rest. At the time of the exodus from Egypt, the destroyer was to go through the whole land and the eldest child in every home was to die. The Israelites, as well as the Egyptians, would suffer the same fate, but the Lord put a 'distinction between Egypt and Israel' (Exod. 11:7). The distinction was the blood of the Passover lamb on the doorframes of their homes. When the judgement came, God said he would pass over those sheltering under the mark of the blood.

The mark of grace means salvation. God said to the six with the deadly weapons 'do not touch anyone who has the mark' (Ezek. 9:6). The mark is a token of ownership that the Christian will never lose. Even in heaven it will still be there. We read in the last chapter of the Bible of the saints in heaven that 'they will see his face, and his name will be on their foreheads' (Rev. 22:4).

The six destroyers have not yet come, but Jesus is already at work. He looks into each heart to see one's attitude to sin. Will he see indifference masquerading under the cloak of being modern? Will he see a casual attitude towards God and his Word? If so, there will be no mark and we are left only with judgement. Will he see a heart grieving over its own sin and the sin of the nation? Will he see repentance and hear the cry for mercy? If so, then he puts upon those the mark of grace, and there will be no judgement.

Even in judgement there is grace, but there is no grace for those who continue in their sin and rejection of God.

FOR FURTHER STUDY

1. Read the account of the first Passover in Exod. 12:1-30.

2. The blood of Christ, that is, the life of Christ, is that which saves sinners (his life lived on their behalf, keeping all of God's law perfectly) and which washes their sins away. Look up the following references in context: 1 Cor. 5:7; Rom. 3:25; 1 John 1:7.

TO THINK ABOUT AND DISCUSS

1. Salvation for sinners was accomplished by the outpouring of the life of the Son of God who lived and died in our place. Our salvation was accomplished at immense expense (1 Peter 1:18-19). Read 1 Peter 4:17-18 and discuss how our lives should show that we have been brought into a right relationship with God.

2. Look up Eph. 4:17-5:7 and mention the specific areas in which it is possible for believers to demonstrate the grace of God as being actively at work in their lives.

5 Whitewashed walls

Ezekiel Chapter 13

Chapter 13 shows how importantly God regards the truth and how strongly he opposes those who deny or distort his word. He calls them false prophets and says in verse 8, 'I am against you.'

It is a frightening thing when Almighty God makes such a strong pronouncement as this. But false teaching is not simply a matter of one man's opinion against another man's opinion; it is a rejection of what God has said, and it involves an open revolt against divine authority. It challenges God with respect to his place on the throne of the universe. It says that God is wrong and therefore is, in fact, not the all-knowing God of Scripture.

False prophets have always troubled the people of God. It was so both in Old and New Testament days and they are still with us today. We are living in days when people believe there is no such thing as absolute truth about God; rather, there is, only opinion. This is nothing new, and it should be remembered how contemptuously Pontius Pilate asked Jesus, 'What is truth?' The answer of Scripture to that is very clear: Jesus said that he is the truth (John 14:6), and the same might be said of God—'Your word is truth' (John 17:17).

Right and wrong

There was a time when everyone knew what was right and wrong. Society had standards that were recognized even if they were not always adhered to. But today all that has changed. Morality has died and 'anything goes' has become the dominant philosophy by which our nation is living, or perhaps more accurately, the philosophy by which it is dying. There is now no such thing as right and wrong, because there are no recognized absolute standards. So, what was condemned thirty years ago, matters such as homosexuality, adultery, public nudity, foul language, etc., are now acceptable. And to want to return to the old standards is regarded by much of society with total intolerance as being puritanical.

Why has this change come about? Has there developed a more loving and gentle spirit in the land? No. The change is the result of a rejection of God and the Christian faith. It is not an expression of love but rather an intolerance of anything that is biblical. For years it was thought that we could have the morality of the New Testament without the Christ of the New Testament. People would say that Christian doctrine was divisive, and all we really needed was the Sermon on the Mount. And now, even the Sermon on the Mount is regarded as too narrow and restrictive.

We need to start by accepting that God's standards are absolute. For instance, what the Lord declared in the Ten Commandments thousands of years ago is still true today. It is still wrong to commit adultery or to covet. Moral truth is not to be dictated by the passing whims of society, but is to be seen as the unchanging will of God. It may be that the world will never accept this, but the Christian must. Our standards must be the ones set out by God in the Bible, otherwise the Christian faith has no authoritative voice with which to speak to the world. A Christian faith which does not practise Christianity is nothing less than hypocrisy.

> Moral truth is not to be dictated by the passing whims of society, but is to be seen as the unchanging will of God.

Conscience is the God-given ability imparted to all men and women to enable them to distinguish between right and wrong. Paul argues that this is equally true of the unbeliever as it is of the believer (Rom. 2:15). Men and women are not animals, and they have more than instinct with which to react to situations. They have a mind and will, and conscience uses these. Conscience is to the mind what pain is to the body; it warns that something is wrong and needs to be dealt with. But the conscience is not infallible and it needs a standard to refer to. The great problem of our nation today is that, having rejected God and the authority of the Bible, its standard of right and wrong is not very high. This is true not just of criminals but of society as a whole, and thus we tolerate moral filth in our homes via

TV that would have been utterly unacceptable thirty years ago. This inevitably blunts the conscience.

The conscience is meant to make us aware of personal guilt but today we are urged to avoid feeling guilty. This often leads to society giving more sympathy to the criminal than to its victim. By its abysmally low standard of right and wrong, and its refusal to accept guilt, society has effectively silenced the conscience.

The Christian's standard has to be the unchanging Word of God. Submission to the authority of Scripture in our everyday lives is the means by which sanctification is worked in us. The purpose of sanctification is to make us like Christ. This is God's desire for us and it ought to be the chief ambition of every believer. It is not easy and it will be totally impossible if our standards are not the same as Christ's. So we need to learn to think biblically and so to absorb the teaching of the Bible that it permeates our thinking and governs our desires. In this way, the conscience has the highest possible standard to relate to.

When the Bible becomes our standard, we shall start to take God seriously and only then will it be possible to take sin seriously. This will enable us to recognize our weaknesses and deal with them. We will be unable to tolerate what God hates. The greatest danger in the Christian life is that we accept our sins as being inevitable. If we believe we can do nothing about our sin, our doctrine of sanctification will be hopelessly wrong because we are told very clearly in Romans 6 that we are dead to sin and we are not to let it reign in our bodies. Sin is no longer our master. Therefore, it cannot compel us to do anything. Sin can only operate in the

Christian if the Christian allows it to.

Withdrawing that co-operation is what the Bible calls putting sin to death. This is an obligation for all believers (Rom. 8:12-13).

The mark of a false prophet

The mark of a false prophet is that he ignores the claims of Jesus, scorns the Bible, and presents his own ideas as the word of God. God says they 'prophesy out of their own imagination' (Ezek. 13:2). These people may be charming, delightful, pleasant and even sincere, but God is against them because of the horrific damage they do.

We see in verse 22 that the damage is two-fold. *Firstly*, they dishearten true believers. This they do by their attacks on Scripture and by denying the Christian's personal experience of salvation. If that is not bad enough, *secondly*, they encourage the wicked to continue in their sin. They teach that we are all children of God, that there is no judgement or hell, and there is no need to be born again because we are all going to heaven. The Authorized Version's rendering of Ezekiel 13:22 suggests that they 'promise life' to unbelievers. Have you ever been to a funeral when you know that the person being buried has lived all his life in defiance of God, and yet the minister stands over his grave and says that he is buried 'in sure and certain hope of resurrection unto life'? It is a lie. If he died without Christ, hell, not heaven, is where he has gone.

False prophets teach lies, says God. It is not that they are somewhat confused, but that they are liars. To say that all religions lead to God is a lie because Jesus said that he alone is the way to God (John 14:6). God says in verse 10 that 'they lead my people astray, saying, "Peace," when there is no peace...' God says there is no peace for the wicked, but the false prophet argues that we are not to take this seriously. It was exactly the same tactic Satan used with Eve in the Garden of Eden.

Thousands of people are being lulled into a false sense of security with such reasonable sounding words as, 'My God would never send anyone to hell.' They say, 'The God I believe in is not the angry God of the Old Testament, but the loving, forgiving God whom Jesus taught about. He is the Father of all mankind and we are all his children. Therefore, there is no such place as hell, and everyone, irrespective of his or her beliefs or actions, will go to heaven.'

> False prophets teach lies, says God. It is not that they are somewhat confused, but that they are liars. To say that all religions lead to God is a lie because Jesus said that he alone is the way to God (John 14:6).

Such a concept of a harmless, affable God would be a great comfort to any unrepentant sinner but, unfortunately for that person, he is not real.

- He is not the God of the Bible;
- He is not the God and Father of the Lord Jesus Christ;
- He is merely the creation of the mind of man and is far removed from the real God whom Jesus revealed to us.

The first messages preached by Jesus, John the Baptist, Peter and Paul all commanded the people to repent. Repentance is of prime importance because men and women and boys and girls are sinners. We are guilty of breaking the commands of God and we need to realize this, turn from our sin, and seek God's forgiveness. Sin is a terrible reality and God will not ignore it. He sent Jesus into this world to save his people from sin and the consequence of sin, which is hell. It is the height of folly for people to say that God will not do certain things when, in the Bible, he clearly says that he will.

We need to accept the complete revelation of God that we find in Scripture, and not just choose pieces we like and reject the rest.

Whitewash

To illustrate the work of the false prophet, God used the picture of a whitewashed wall (Ezek. 13:10). False teachers always bypass the question of people's sin and guilt—they do a whitewash job. The wall referred to was probably the city wall which was vital in protecting the people from their enemies. They built flimsy walls—easy to erect, cheap, quick to put up, but useless. The builders knew this, but, to cover up the deficiency of their work, they gave the wall a coat of whitewash. This made the flimsy wall look attractive but God's verdict was that it was 'going to fall' (Ezek. 13:11).

> False teachers always bypass the question of people's sin and guilt ...

We see the application of this principle everywhere. People are encouraged to build flimsy walls of their own self-righteousness; easy religion and sentimental doctrines are the order of our day; there should always be a feeling of wellbeing, so nothing must be said that could cause sinners to feel guilt or conviction. Consequently, people have come to think of the church as some sort of emotional aspirin to make them feel good. Nothing, they say, must be allowed to disturb their spiritual and moral sleep.

It is all whitewash. It is a refusal to face the reality that people are building flimsy lives which are unacceptable to God. This is why the age-old doctrine of salvation by works, which the New Testament vigorously denies, is so popular. This makes it easy to reject the gospel call for repentance. There are multitudes of whitewashed souls that, from the outside, look nice and respectable, affable and kind, but whose hearts remain fundamentally unchanged. The trouble with whitewash is that it wears off. It washes away and has to be done again and again.

The answer

When I was a boy at the end of the Second World War, I lived in a terrace house that really was a slum. We only had one room upstairs and one room downstairs that could be used. Our small back yard was covered with flagstones and surrounded by a high wall. In the far corner of the yard was our only toilet, so we used the yard every day. The walls, like the house, were crumbling and decaying, so, to keep it reasonably tidy, my father would give it a coat of whitewash every year. When this was done it looked fresh and sparkling, but we knew it only covered up the decaying walls.

This went on for years until the local authority condemned the house as unfit to live in and moved us out into a new prefabricated building. Then there was no need for whitewash.

Isn't that like many lives? Spiritually they are decaying and crumbling, and God says, 'I condemn that life.' They may seem to be morally impeccable, but spiritually they are a slum. However, the God who condemns us is also willing to move us out and provide a new life for us in Christ. He is a God who does not whitewash, but washes us clean in the blood of his Son.

How can a condemned, sin-polluted life stand before the unblinking holiness of God? They may not know the hymn but all repentant sinners know the feelings of Thomas Binney.

Eternal Light! Eternal Light!
How pure the soul must be,
When, placed within thy searching sight,
It shrinks not, but with calm delight
Can live and look on thee.

O how shall I, whose native sphere
Is dark, whose mind is dim,
Before the Ineffable appear,
And on my naked spirit bare
The uncreated beam?

There is a way for man to rise
To that sublime abode;
An offering and a sacrifice,
A Holy Spirit's energies,
An Advocate with God.

This is God's answer to whitewash. This is God's way of salvation. The answer is Jesus. He came into the world to deal with our sin and guilt. When he died on the cross and shed his blood, it was an act of atoning grace. He was paying the debt we owed for all our violations of the law of God. The result of Calvary is that the blood of Jesus cleanses us from all sin. God demolishes the old life and gives us new life in Christ.

For further study ▶

FOR FURTHER STUDY

1. Look up Deut. 13, and note how seriously false prophecy was to be taken by the people of Israel. Compare this section with Deut. 18:17-22.

2. The Lord Jesus warned of false prophets, both by his own words and through the apostles (see Matt. 7:15-20 and Acts 20:29-31). Look up these passages and note the characteristics of a false prophet.

3. Compare John 14:6 and Acts 4:10-12 and note the clear teaching of the New Testament with regard to the exclusivity of Christ as Saviour.

TO THINK ABOUT AND DISCUSS

1. Some radio stations and TV channels offer short religious broadcasts—mini devotionals or epilogues, etc. Some of these may be led by godly ministers, but others may be led by false prophets. Think of one or two such messages and analyse the elements which showed whether the speaker was a true believer or a false prophet.

2. The Lord Jesus taught clearly about the importance of building our lives on the strong foundation of the rock (see Matt. 7:24-27). Do you know of people who have ignored his counsel? How did this become apparent in their lives? How, in practice, would you encourage others (perhaps your children or a friend) to build their lives on the foundation that Jesus taught about?

6 The heart of man

Ezekiel Chapter 16

In the visions Ezekiel has received, he is shown a great deal about the human heart. When God speaks of the heart, he is not referring to the pump in one's chest that is so essential to life, but to the heart as the centre of one's will, desires and emotions. Nevertheless the physical heart is used to give spiritual parallels to the condition of men and women.

In Ezekiel 16:1-14, God describes his love for his people in a most vivid and intimate way. The mercies and goodness of God to mankind are staggering as verses 10-14 particularly show. God says, '... the splendour I have given you made your beauty perfect.'

Then in verse. 15 we read 'But' and there follows a description of mankind's total ingratitude and rebellion against his God. As God views all this, his reaction to people in sin is 'How weak-willed you are' (v. 30), or, as the *New King James Version* renders it, 'How degenerate is your heart.' The problem is a person's heart. It is degenerate, weak, stubborn and rebellious.

A sick heart

The specialist in hospital told me that my heart was in a serious condition. How did he know? First of all, he was guided by the symptoms—pain, tightening of the chest, breathlessness and an inability to do ordinary things. There is so much heart trouble today and many will recognize these symptoms, but thankfully most people do not suffer in this way.

> God says that we all have a serious heart condition, and in the Bible he spells out the symptoms.

But God says that we *all* have a serious heart condition, and in the Bible he spells out the symptoms:

The heart is deceitful above all things
and beyond cure.
Who can understand it?
(Jer. 17:9).

For out of the heart come evil thoughts, murder, adultery, sexual immorality, theft, false testimony, slander. These are what make a man 'unclean'…
(Matt. 15:18-20).

Our sins are the evidence of our heart condition. Sin always brings pain; it appears to be enjoyable but it always ends in unhappiness. Sin brings breathlessness, an absence of the life-giving breath of the Holy Spirit. Sin renders us unable to do the things we were created for—to love and serve God.

If a heart specialist told you that you had a serious heart condition, you would be a fool to ignore it. What is your reaction to God's diagnosis of your heart? Do you take it seriously? Are you anxious for a cure?

In my case, having considered the symptoms, the doctor then examined my heart more closely. A painless and fascinating technique enabled him to show me my own heart on a video monitor and point out to me what was wrong and what needed to be done.

> If a heart specialist told you that you had a serious heart condition, you would be a fool to ignore it.

God shows us our heart. He knows the exact condition it is in. Often we may look all right on the surface; morally and socially we seem to be very acceptable—but how does *God* see us? He often speaks of the heart of man in the Bible. There we read that the apostle Peter told a respectable man that, in God's sight, his heart was not right (Acts 8:21). The same is true of us all.

The heart specialist will cite things like smoking cigarettes, having a wrong diet and lack of exercise as the main causes of heart problems. Spiritually, our heart problems are caused by sin, which is a rejection of God's ways. The medical consultant told me that the only answer was *surgery*, that my problem was a blockage of the arteries, and that this had to be dealt with to allow the blood to do its job of taking oxygen to my heart. Therefore I needed a bypass operation and this would involve the surgeon taking a vein from the leg and using it to bypass the blockage in the artery, thus allowing a full flow of life-giving blood.

This was the only answer to my heart problem. And the only answer to the *spiritual* need of all our hearts is for the blood of Jesus Christ to do its work of bringing forgiveness and life. What Jesus did for us on the cross is the *only* thing that can make sinners clean in God's sight.

Our problem is *sin*. It pollutes the heart and makes us unacceptable to God. But Jesus came into the world to deal with sin. He did this once and for all on the cross, by taking the punishment our sins deserved. *He died in our place.* That is why the Bible speaks of salvation through his blood. Morality, religion and education are no remedy for our heart condition. The only answer acceptable to God is *Jesus*.

A divided heart

God says, 'I will give them an undivided heart and put a new spirit in them; I will remove from them their heart of stone and give them a heart of flesh' (Ezek. 11:19). Man's trouble is not his head—an ignorance of the truth, but his heart—a rejection of the truth. David prays in Psalm 86:11, 'Give me an undivided heart that I may fear your name.' Human nature gives us all hearts in opposition to God. Our hearts are divided by sin so that we are not interested in what God wants. When we become Christians, our hearts of stone are replaced with hearts of flesh that begin to respond to God's Word. But sadly, before long, disobedience may creep in and our hearts become divided between pleasing God and pleasing self.

This divided heart needs to be changed so that it is undivided in its commitment to God. How does God do this? He has to perform a divine operation. Have you ever purchased an electrical gadget that has gone wrong? You send for the technician but, when he comes, he tells you the job is too big for him to do in your home, and that he will have to take the malfunctioning gadget away. 'Give me your vacuum cleaner,' he says, 'and I will return it to you as good as new.'

> **God … has to perform a divine operation…**

This is only a poor illustration of what God means when he asks believers to give him their hearts. He says, 'I will deal with it and return it to you as an undivided heart.' In other words, we come to God asking him to give to us, and at the same time we give to him. We surrender our will to the divine will. We empty our hearts of self, but this is only possible when there is a true loathing of personal sin and a deep longing to please God. See how Charles Wesley puts it:

> Let earth no more my heart divide,
> With Christ may I be crucified,
> To thee with my whole soul aspire;
> Dead to the world and all its toys,
> Its idle pomp, and fading joys,
> Be thou alone my one desire.

My will be swallowed up in thee;
Light in my light still may I see,
Beholding thee with open face;
Called the full power of faith to prove,
Let all my hallowed heart in love,
And all my ransomed life be praise.

God's heart

The only answer to the sin and depravity of the heart of mankind is the abundance of love and grace there is in the heart of God. It is not difficult to describe the heart of mankind because we all know it, but how do we begin to describe the heart of God?

God's heart beats with a depth of compassion that is beyond human understanding. This does not mean it is blind to our sin. In the terrible description of people in sin in Ezekiel 16:15-59, God uses words like 'prostitution', 'detestable', 'promiscuity', 'lewd', 'weak-willed' and 'brazen', to describe people's rebellion. But in spite of this when we reach verse 60, we read the word 'yet'—in other words, there is still mercy available.

God ... is not blind to our sin ...

Here is the depth of God's love. If he were to deal with us as we deserve, there would be no hope. The word 'yet' holds out hope for us. This is further strengthened in Ezekiel 18 with the heart of God pleading with sinners, 'Rid yourselves of all the offences you have committed, and get a new heart and a new spirit. Why will you die, O house of Israel? For I take no pleasure in the death of anyone, declares the Sovereign LORD. Repent and live!' (vv. 31-32).

Then there is the promise of God, 'I will sprinkle clean water on you, and you will be clean; I will cleanse you from all your impurities and from all your idols. I will give you a new heart and put a new spirit in you; I will remove from you your heart of stone and give you a heart of flesh. And I will put my Spirit in you and move you to follow my decrees and be careful to keep my laws. You will live in the land I gave your forefathers; you will be my people, and I will be your God. I will save you from all your uncleanness' (Ezek. 36:25-29). Who but a loving God could be so gracious as this?

> The greatest heart specialist, God himself, has diagnosed the condition of your heart.

The heart of God is open to us. His pleadings and promises can leave no doubt that there is mercy with him for sinners.

The greatest heart specialist, God himself, has diagnosed the condition of your heart.

- It is serious.
- It is fatal.
- It is terminal.
- *You need a new heart.*

God does not do bypass operations; *his surgery is much more radical.*

According to the Bible, he takes away the stony heart—the one that is blocked, hard and unresponsive to God—and gives a new one!

God will give this to you when you turn away from your sin and, with your whole being, trust in the Lord Jesus.

FOR FURTHER STUDY

1. In Scripture, the theme of 'heart' is a major one. Look up the following references and note how the human heart has become corrupted in so many ways: Jer. 17:9-10; 1 Sam. 16:7; Ps. 14:1; Prov. 12:20; Matt. 15:8.

2. Look up Prov. 4:23 and suggest how Ps. 51:17 and Ezek. 11:9 relate to it.

TO THINK ABOUT AND DISCUSS

1. If sin begins in the heart, explain why the gospel is so radical in the cure it brings to the human condition.

2. Some evangelistic approaches seem only to address the intellect and will of an unconverted person. In what ways does such an approach need to be modified and improved in order to take into consideration the fallenness and desperate wickedness of the heart as has been explained in this chapter?

7 A new heart

Ezekiel Chapter 36

The previous section has considered the desperate condition of the human heart—we now turn our attention to Ezekiel's teaching on God's cure for the human heart described in chapter 36.

The promise of God in Ezekiel 36:25-26 is to give us a new heart. The way God deals with men and women has changed little from Ezekiel's day to ours because people do not change. Certainly, in 2,500 years there have been many outward changes, but basically mankind is still the same—people's hearts have not changed. God is concerned with our hearts, not with our intellect or culture or scientific progress. Current events prove this. All the great strides forward in popular education and all the benefits of affluence of recent years have not been able to prevent the breakdown of family life, the plague of broken marriages, battered children, and the general increase in crime. In spite of all the scientific knowledge amassed in the past one hundred years, we cannot prevent wars, we cannot find work for millions of people, and we cannot cure the racial hatred and distrust that abounds in our cities.

A defiled land

In this chapter, God is speaking to a people he has blessed in remarkable ways, yet a people who have spurned him. He accuses them of defiling the land (Ezek. 36:17). This they did by their conduct and their action of ignoring God.

Isn't that equally true of our nation? The blessings of God on Britain over the centuries are beyond description. The spiritual blessings that came with the Protestant Reformation have enriched every part of our lives—the English Bible and the culture that flowed from that; the wealth of Christian literature in English; and the political freedom we have enjoyed so that no enemy has invaded us since 1066. Very few nations have known such mercies!

Yet today, we are godless, pagan and unbelieving because we have rejected God. Instead of putting our trust in him, we have put our hope in politicians, and they have all proved inadequate. It was not so long ago that a British Home Secretary said that the 'permissive society' was the 'civilized society'.

> Today, we are godless, pagan and unbelieving because we have rejected God.

But now everyone can see that the permissive society has eroded all standards of moral behaviour and self-discipline. The defilement of the land has been going on for years in

Parliament with trendy MPs who will do anything for votes; in our schools where teachers are not allowed to discipline the children; and in our homes with broken marriages and fragmented families. We have created a monster and it is beginning to devour us!

There is no answer for all this from the politicians and sociologists because the problem is the heart of mankind. Only God can deal with that.

A heart of stone

What does God mean when he says that a person has a heart of stone? He is referring to human nature defiled by sin, and he says there is nothing to be done with it. It cannot be repaired; it must be scrapped and replaced with a heart of flesh.

The politician cannot understand this, the sociologist refuses to believe it, and the humanist angrily rejects it; they all try to patch up what God has condemned as beyond repair. Human nature cannot be mended. It is not like an old house that can be put right with a grant from the council. It is rotten throughout; its foundation is gone and every timber is worm-ridden.

> What a person needs is a new heart, a new spirit and a new nature.

This is why God makes no attempt to repair it. He will not shore up the walls or repair the roof. He will not repair it—it needs to be replaced. What a person needs is a new heart, a new spirit and a new nature.

It could be objected that this is a very pessimistic view of human nature. But is it really? Consider a person from God's viewpoint. He made man and put him in Paradise. Yet it was in Paradise that man rejected God. It was neither in a slum, nor in a socially deprived environment—but in Paradise! That sin of rejecting God then dominates all that man does. Before long Cain is killing his brother Abel and then in Genesis 6:5 we read, 'The LORD saw how great man's wickedness on the earth had become, and that every inclination of the thoughts of his heart was only evil all the time.'

The same result of sin can be seen throughout history right up until the time Jesus came. God sent his Son and men crucified him. Here is the depth of human sin, but it did not finish there, and all through the centuries it has dominated our thinking and actions. This is the general picture of human nature. From time to time there are spots of light, of kindness and integrity, but generally it is a picture of man without God— man with a heart of stone.

> God does not want to leave us in the mess we have created for ourselves...

A heart of flesh

God does not want to leave us in the mess we have created for ourselves but is willing to replace the heart of stone with a heart of flesh. In other words, he is willing to give us a new nature that delights in him and is able to respond to his directions. He does this not because we deserve it, but as an act of grace. In fact, God clearly says, 'I want you to know that I am not doing this for your sake' (Ezek. 36:32).

A heart of flesh in exchange for a heart of stone suggests a change so radical and profound that no one but God could do it. Jesus likens it to being born again (John 3:3, 7) and Paul compares it to a new creation (2 Cor. 5:17). Neither of these phrases is too extravagant because the change God works in human nature is miraculous.

In this change of natures there are several distinct events, some of which are mentioned in Ezekiel 36.

·**RESTORATION TO GOD** (v. 24). The reference is to the nation being brought back from Babylon to Israel. But it is also a picture of a spiritual change. For instance, the prodigal son was brought back from a foreign land to his father. All sinners are aliens to God and need to be reconciled to him.

·**CLEANSING FROM SIN** (vv. 25-26). This is crucial. Sin separates us from God and has to be dealt with. God only cleanses from sin on the basis of Jesus dying to pay the debt our sin has incurred. Notice in verse 25 that all sin is dealt with—past, present and future—by the death of Jesus.

·**THE INDWELLING OF THE HOLY SPIRIT** (v. 27). There is a new lordship with a new direction of life and a new power given us to live our lives to the glory of God. The Holy Spirit enables us to understand the things of God and gives us a desire to want to obey God. This is far more than a person merely becoming religious.

·**THERE IS A NEW RELATIONSHIP TO GOD** (v. 28). One of the greatest privileges is to know that we are the people of God. We are no longer his enemies but his children.

·**A LOATHING OF SIN** (v. 31). There is a completely new attitude to sin. Being a Christian does not mean that we never sin again, but when we do, we will hate that sin and long to be free from it.

For further study ▶

FOR FURTHER STUDY

1. Isa. 1: 5 and Gen. 6:5 portray people in very negative terms, and yet Jer. 24:7 and Ezek. 11:19 promise good things to those whose hearts God renews. Look up each of these passages in its context.

2. Look up the following passages in the New Testament: John 1:12-13; John 3:5-7; 2 Cor. 5:17. Summarize what they teach about the new birth.

TO THINK ABOUT AND DISCUSS

1. The Bible gives counsel to us in regard to keeping the heart—see Prov. 4:23. What are some of the difficulties that a person is likely to experience in guarding his or her heart from sin. Consider this in the light of:

- Human relationships;
- Possessions and material trappings;
- Thought-life;
- Use of the tongue;
- Response to the media.

2. As believers, we aim to live a life of perseverance in holiness, but we do so with divine help! Look up the following references: Jude 1; 2 Peter 2:4-9; Rom. 8:31-39. How do these demonstrate the keeping power of God? How could you cultivate a greater sense of reliance on the Lord for his help in the areas of life in which you face difficulties from week to week?

8 Wrong views of God

Ezekiel Chapter 18

Most men and women have very definite views about God. They may not call themselves religious, go to church or read the Bible, but their views about God are held firmly and sometimes most tenaciously.

It seems that everyone is entitled to believe what he or she wants to believe about God. Subjective feelings and old wives' tales are given as much authority as the Bible in this matter. It is quite incredible, but also inevitable, once the authority of Scripture is rejected.

There are basically only two views about God we can have: either the biblical view, that is, God's revealed truth, or a viewpoint created by our own imagination. We saw in Ezekiel 13 that false Christianity does not take God seriously and therefore cannot take sin seriously because it prophesies out of its own imagination (v. 2).

Most people will reject the biblical teaching because it always shows them and their sin in a very bad light. So they concoct views of God that excuse their sin or that play it down. Such views include the idea that, because God is love, there is therefore no wrath, no judgement of sin and no hell. That is not what the Bible teaches, but it is a convenient belief for the person who has no intention of repenting and turning from his or her sin. The only trouble is that it is completely wrong—it is self-deception in a grand manner.

Our understanding of the character of God is crucial and we just must get it right. If you had a choice of two weeks' holiday in the best hotel in Bermuda, with all expenses paid, or the option of spending two weeks in a caravan on a traffic island in the East End of London, which would you take? In the short term your choice is important because the quality of your holiday and your enjoyment depend upon it. But, in the long term, it does not matter because you will be home again in two weeks!

> Our understanding of the character of God is crucial and we just must get it right.

Now imagine a man driving down a straight road at extremely high speed; he comes to a fork in the road. If he goes to the right, it leads to a better road that goes on for miles, but if he goes to the left, he will suddenly find the road dropping down a vast precipice to rocks below. In both the short term or the long term his choice matters because there is no coming back and there is no second chance. He must get it right or die. So it is also with our beliefs about God. We must get it right: heaven or hell depends on this.

Excuses and examples

In Ezekiel 18 we read of people with wrong views of God. These people, 2,500 years ago, were just like us today and objected to being told that they were sinners under the wrath of God. They were in Babylon because of their sin and they were experiencing the judgement of God. But even this did not cause them to take God seriously or learn from their past mistakes.

Today our nation is in moral decline. The picture is one of total moral chaos and decay. No one doubts this, but we object to being told it is all a result of our sin. All sorts of excuses are made. The latest popular view is that our behaviour cannot be our fault as our genes dictate our behaviour.

The people in Ezekiel's day had never heard of genes but they had a well-known proverb to excuse themselves:

The fathers eat sour grapes,
and the children's teeth are set on edge
(Ezek. 18:2).

In effect, this said that God cannot blame us because it is our parents' fault. On the surface, this may seem a reasonable argument. For instance, many young people growing up today have few moral or behavioural standards. Most have never been to church or ever even opened a Bible, but, on the contrary, they are exposed to all sorts of moral filth in their homes through the TV, videos, books and magazines. It is more difficult for a teenager in Britain today to hear the truth about God than it was fifty years ago, and, up to a point, it is the fault of previous generations. The religious and moral rot of today started a hundred years ago. So does that excuse today's teenagers? No, because God holds each individual responsible for his or her sins. 'The soul who sins is the one who will die' (vv. 4, 20).

To show the truth of this, God gives three examples:

·**THE EXAMPLE OF A GOOD MAN** and the consequences of his goodness—vv. 5-9;

·**THE EXAMPLE OF THE GOOD MAN'S SON** who rejects all that his father has stood for and leads a sinful life. Such a life also has its consequences—vv. 10-13;

·**THE EXAMPLE OF THE EVIL MAN'S SON** who sees all that is wrong in his father's life and lives a good life himself. This too has its consequences—vv. 14-18.

The clear meaning of the three examples is that each of us is personally responsible to God. Your parents may be good or bad. The influences upon your life may be good or bad, but still your sin is your own responsibility. Your upbringing, though very important, is not the governing factor. The problem is the human heart where the root of all sin lies.

God's way

Man's view is that sin is not a serious problem. After all, it is argued, God cannot expect more from us than that we try our best. So there is created the super-pious idea that the good-living, respectable person deserves the favour of God, whereas others deserve all that is coming to them. With such thinking rooted in the human mind, it is impossible then to understand the ways of God. So God's way is dismissed as unfair.

Ezekiel 18:21-32 is an important passage and blends in perfectly with the New Testament teaching on salvation. How can a man be right with God? How can he know he is saved and be sure of eternal life? Derek Thomas has written:

> It must be made clear that in all these examples, Ezekiel is not suggesting that the 'righteous' man obtains the reward of life on the basis of what he has done alone. In order to follow a life of obedience, Ezekiel makes it clear that a man needs a 'new heart and a new spirit' (v. 31). Before Jesus ever told Nicodemus that he needed to be born again (or from above) in order to obtain the life that the kingdom of heaven offered, the Old Testament prophets had spoken of the very same necessity. The fact is that those who demonstrate a life of obedience, and are therefore assured of the life of glory, are those who have turned from their sin to God (v. 21). 'When we discuss the cause of salvation we must look nowhere else but the mercy of God, and there we must stop.' (John Calvin). [10]

God says to us through Ezekiel that if we trust our own goodness and morality as a basis of salvation, we are always on precarious ground. One sin is enough to condemn us. Our emotional response to that may be to argue that this is unfair, but a more reasoned response would be to see the utter fallacy of trusting our own goodness because there, mingled with all our righteousness, is sin; with our helping hand goes pride; with our congratulation of others there is envy; covetousness, jealousy and gossip are mingled with everything we do, simply because human nature is corrupt and defiled. Some may think that this is a very pessimistic view, but it is simply what God says. The person who thinks he or she is good enough for God just does not understand his or her own heart, and certainly has no concept of the holiness of God.

The only way to be acceptable to God is God's way, and God's way starts with repentance. The Lord applies this truth to a person who has lived a rotten life (vv. 27-28). The wages of sin is death but God has no pleasure in that (v. 32). He is a God of infinite love and mercy and is willing to forgive all sin, yet it must be on his terms. This is because sin has grieved his holy character and violated his holy law. Sin deserves death and hell, but God pleads with the sinner to turn from his or her sin, to repent, and come to him for a new heart. We should repent because our sin is taking us to hell. But there is more to it than that: we must also see that our sin grieves God, so, as well as seeking forgiveness, we should also long for a new heart to enable us to live for the glory of God. Our sin is able to be dealt with by the atoning death of Jesus on the cross and, because of this, God is able to cry from his heart, 'Why will you die?' (v. 31). There is no need to die because there is salvation available.

> The only way to be acceptable to God is God's way, and God's way starts with repentance.

- **ALL SIN DESERVES HELL**—that is fair;
- **ALL SIN CAN BE FORGIVEN**—that is grace;
- **AND GRACE IS FAIR**, or a better word would be 'just', because our sin is judged, condemned and punished at the cross.

For further study ▶

FOR FURTHER STUDY

1. Look up the following Bible references on the purity of God, and summarize their message on the holiness of God in one or two sentences: Deut. 32:4; Job 34:10; Hab 1:13.

2. Note how the Bible teaches the universality of sin—the fact that there is nobody exempt from bring a sinner—in the following passages: Ps. 143:2; Prov. 20:9; Rom. 3:23; 1 John 1:8-10.

TO THINK ABOUT AND DISCUSS

1. In the *Westminster Confession of Faith*, God is described in these words:
'There is but one only living, and true God, who is infinite in being and perfection, a most pure spirit, invisible, without body, parts, or passions; immutable, immense, eternal, incomprehensible, almighty, most wise, most holy, most free, most absolute; working all things according to the counsel of his own immutable and most righteous will, for his own glory; most loving, gracious, merciful, long-suffering, abundant in goodness and truth, forgiving iniquity, transgression, and sin; the rewarder of them that diligently seek him; and withal, most just, and terrible in his judgements, hating all sin, and who will by no means clear the guilty.'
Discuss this description of God in the light of views of God that are commonly held and expressed today.

2. Self-deception has been described as 'the gentle art'. People deceive themselves with seriously wrong views of God and of salvation. Outline two or three such views that you know of in the world today. How could you help such misled people come to a clear view of the truth of the gospel?

9 Coming judgement

Ezekiel Chapter 22

Everything the Lord told Ezekiel to do was meant as a lesson for Judah. Even the prophet's grief at the coming judgement was used in this way. In chapter 20:45-49, the prophet is told of this judgement. Babylon will come from the north and attack Judah—the forest of the southland. The judgement will be devastating and it is made clear that 'I the Lord have kindled it.'

This was not just a case of one nation attacking another, but very definitely the judgement of God. The people were oblivious to this and Ezekiel thought that even if they knew it, they would not take it seriously—'Isn't he just telling parables?' (v. 49). But the prophet knew the truth and he must have felt it deeply in his heart. These were his people and he did not want to see them dealt with like this, even though they deserved it. The Lord had told him not to hide his feelings but to 'groan before them with broken heart and bitter grief' (Ezek. 21:6). He was to let them see that he, at least, took God's judgement seriously. Then they would ask questions and give the prophet an opportunity to tell them what would happen.

The people seemed to have been in a spiritual stupor. They listened eagerly to the false prophets who promised them peace, so consequently no one took sin seriously (Ezek. 22:28-29). A result of this was that no one saw the need to pray for the nation. God lamented, 'I looked for a man among them who would build up the wall and stand before me in the gap on behalf of the land so I would not have to destroy it, but I found none' (Ezek. 22:30).

The coming judgement was clearly a result of the people's sin—but with our God there is always mercy and forgiveness. The problem was that there was no repentance because they did not recognize their sin.

If there is no conviction of sin, there can be no repentance, and if there is no repentance, there will be no forgiveness. The recognition of our true state before God is absolutely crucial for salvation. Therefore it is vital in evangelism that men and women be confronted with their sin, and God has given us the law to accomplish the needed conviction.

> The recognition of our true state before God is absolutely crucial for salvation.

The Law and conviction of sin

The law that God gave to Israel at Sinai, by the hand of Moses, is a verbal expression of the holiness of his character.

It puts into words what God is like, and what God expects. Thus when the law says, 'You shall have no gods before me' (Exod. 20:3, Deut. 5:7), it is not evidence of petty resentment on the part of God, but of holy jealousy. God demands our sole obedience because all other gods are false gods and will lead us astray. The law, then, is *restrictive* only in order to be *protective*. It is for our good, or, to put it another way, it expresses both God's holiness and his love. It is impossible to preach a full gospel without both these ingredients being present!

> The law is restrictive only in order to be protective.

It is not 'conviction of sin' for a person to feel bad because he or she is drinking too much or generally making a mess of life. Sin is not just a violation of socially accepted standards. To see sin only in social or moral terms will not lead people to conviction. Sin must be seen in the light of the law and holiness of God. The gospel is not an aspirin for the aches of life, to soothe and comfort people in their misery. It is a holy God's answer to the violation of divine law by human beings whose very nature is to rebel against him.

Most people think salvation is the product of morality and religious observance. In spite of the clarity of the New Testament message, they still cling to their own efforts to save themselves. But salvation by works never creates conviction of sin because it fails miserably to take into account the holiness, purity and justice of God. It sees sin only as a moral or social blemish, and not as an affront to the Word, law and character of God. It is the law of God which produces conviction because it shows us our sin in relationship, not to society and people, but to God. It shows us that we have failed to meet God's requirements.

Because we are sinners, the law of God is obnoxious to us, and that is so for two reasons.

The first reason is that the law *is* law, and the sinner does not like being told he or she is wrong. The sinner does not like absolutes but prefers standards that are relative, because such standards can be manipulated to serve his or her own convenience. The absolutes of God's law defy such human ingenuity: they will not appease the conscience and they leave that person forever uncomfortable in the presence of God.

The second reason is that it is the law *of God*. There is a holiness about the law that will not yield in the slightest to a person's sinfulness. It makes no allowances and accepts no plea in mitigation. It is the unchanging law of an unchanging God, and is thus as holy and pure as God himself.

> The sinner does not like absolutes but prefers standards that are relative, because such standards can be manipulated to serve his or her own convenience.

There are only two ways in which a person could come to terms with God's law. The first is if the law could be altered so that it could agree with human sinful inclination. A person would then be happy in sin because the law would become like his or her own heart, and there would be no conflict between that person and law. The second is if mankind could be changed so that the inclinations and desires of his heart would be in accordance with divine law. Then again there would be no conflict.

The first of these two 'options' is not a consideration, but the second is made possible by the gospel of God's grace. However, if the gospel is to have this effect, it must be presented in such a way that makes it clear where the human problem lies. The prime purpose of the gospel is not to make people happy but to make them righteous in the sight of God. Therefore, there is no way the gospel can be preached without the law also being preached. It is only the preaching of the law that shows people what their problem really is, since it is through the law that we become conscious of sin (Rom. 3:20). The law presents us firmly and forcibly with the fact of our own personal sin and guilt (Rom. 3:20; 4:15; 5:13) and having done that, it can lead us in repentance and faith to Christ.

> The prime purpose of the gospel is not to make people happy but to make them righteous in the sight of God.

Telling it as it is

In preaching the law, we must not put before the sinner vague and tentative suggestions as to what God thinks, but clear and precise statements of his attitude to the issues that confront men and women every day. The law leaves us in no doubt as to the holiness of God, and this confronts the sinner with a huge dilemma. What can he do? His sin condemns him; the holiness of God leaves him with no escape. The law

> A man is never so near grace as when he begins to feel he can do nothing at all.

has pushed him into a corner and kicked away the crutches he was depending on. He feels useless and hopeless! But this is the point at which he must arrive if he is to embrace by faith what Christ has done to redeem lost sinners such as he is. The great preacher C. H. Spurgeon once said, 'A man is never so near grace as when he begins to feel he can do nothing at all.'

Dennis Lane has written:

Ezekiel points out in chapter 22 the tragedy of a society in which no one can be found to stand up and be counted (v. 30)… We may feel that our witness is one against the crowd. What is the point of standing against an overwhelming tide? In the Lord's reckoning, the individual counts, even in a day when men discount him and his testimony. One person can make all the difference between life and death, disaster and deliverance. A day of deterioration is a day for boldness, not despair, a day for each one to take a deliberate stand for the Lord.[11]

Telling someone the gospel involves speaking both of the law and the grace of God. No one is saved by hearing the law only, but it is necessary for men and women that they hear this if they are to take their sin seriously. It is grace alone that saves but grace does not work in isolation. The business of the people of God is to tell the world all that God has said. It is certain that they will not like the message but we know that the message of 'peace, peace', by itself, is wrong. God is angry with sin and will deal with it.

We are not only to tell it as it is but to show by our manner and presentation, as Ezekiel had to, that this is a serious matter. If we can speak of hell without deep concern for our hearers, then we are not doing it properly. If we can witness without a sense of urgency, then we ourselves are not taking it seriously.

For further study ▶

FOR FURTHER STUDY

1. Scripture repeatedly makes the point that there is both sternness with God and kindness, too—sternness towards sin, and yet love for sinners. Look up the following references: Rom. 11:22; Luke 13:34; 1 Tim. 2:3-4; 1 Peter 4:18; 2 Peter 3:9.

2. Repentance featured centrally in the message preached by Jesus, John the Baptist and the apostles. Look up the following references: Luke 13:3, 5; Mark 1:4, 14-15; Acts 2:38; Acts 20:21.

TO THINK ABOUT AND DISCUSS

1. It is in the realm of mystery that God both knows the future (and determines what will happen in it) and yet also sincerely urges sinners to repent and trust in the Lord Jesus Christ as he is freely offered in the gospel. As you walk closely with God in prayer and the reading of his Word, how should this affect the way in which you share the gospel?

2. Why do some modern people so despise the Bible's emphasis on repentance when repentance is explained to them in biblical terms?

3. Why do repentance towards God and faith in Christ so often appear together in New Testament teaching? Think of a few ways in which you could incorporate these elements more clearly into the way in which you share the message of the gospel.

10 Spiritual adultery

Ezekiel Chapter 23

Divorce statistics show a dramatic increase worldwide. Few people in our society today remain unaffected as so many relationships become compromised through inappropriate liaisons. The image of adultery is a powerful one, and even more so when it becomes evident that God's people are guilty of this very matter in the spiritual sense.

Ezekiel 23 is very graphic in its description of the relationship that existed between the sisters Oholah and Oholibah and their lovers. The sisters represent the nations of Israel and Judah (v. 4) and the purpose of the chapter is to show us our sin as God sees it. Sin is not a harmless activity a Christian can engage in with no thought as to its consequence. It is true that, for a Christian, all sin—past, present and future—has been dealt with at the cross and there is no condemnation (in the eternal sense). But that does not mean there are no consequences to

face because of our sin. We will not pick up the wages of sin
but we will have to face the stink and pollution that sin
inevitably brings into our lives. We cannot lose our salvation
but we can lose the joy of our salvation and the awareness of
the peace of God.

Another consequence of sin in the lives of those God refers
to in the words, 'they were mine' (v. 4) is that God himself is
deeply grieved. It is folly to protest that our sin hurts no
one—it always hurts God, as Ezekiel 23 so clearly shows.
This is, perhaps, the most important lesson we can learn
from this chapter or even from the
whole book of Ezekiel. How
would you feel if your spouse
committed adultery? That is only a
pale reflection of how God feels
when his bride, the church,
commits spiritual adultery.

> It is folly to protest that our sin hurts no one—it always hurts God.

It is often said that there are no innocent parties in divorce
and it is argued that there has to be fault on both sides.
Whether that is true in human relationships is open to
debate, but when we sin against our God and Saviour, the
guilt is totally on our side. God does nothing to deserve such
unfaithfulness.

Matthew Henry wrote these words on the phrase 'they
were mine':

> They were mine, for they were the seed of Abraham his friend
> and of Jacob his chosen; they were in covenant with God, and
> carried about with them the sign of their circumcision, the
> seal of the covenant. They were mine, and therefore their

apostasy was the highest injustice. It was alienating God's property, it was the basest ingratitude to the best of benefactors, and a perfidious treacherous violation of the most sacred engagements. Note, those who have been in profession the people of God, but who have revolted from him, have a great deal to answer for more than those who never made any such profession.[12]

How God sees our sin

In Ezekiel 23, God describes the sin of his people as prostitution (fourteen times) and adultery (five times). Our problem is that we don't see sin like that. If we saw our worldliness as spiritual prostitution, perhaps we would do something about it. We regard prostitution as something vile and degrading, and we would be appalled if our daughter became a prostitute—yet that is how God sees our pride, anger and gossip. Our sin should shame us but, instead, we pamper it, encourage it, feed it and generally get on very well with it. We can more than tolerate it, but God cannot tolerate it and never will tolerate it.

> Our sin should shame us but, instead, we pamper it ... but God cannot tolerate it and never will tolerate it.

There is a difference between prostitution and adultery. Prostitution is selling your most precious possession to anyone willing to pay the price. There is no lasting or serious relationship involved—it is casual and temporary. Neither is love involved, only a desire for financial gain. This gain is so highly valued that the prostitute is prepared to sell her body to achieve it.

Adultery, however, is giving yourself to someone who has no right to you. It implies a deep relationship with a lover, and a dissatisfaction with one's legitimate marriage partner. It is a denial of all past promises and allegiances, and will involve lies and cover up.

How does this work out in spiritual terms?

Prostitution is the equivalent of worldliness and carnality. It may be seen in the Christian whose relationship with God is shallow. There is no commitment and he or she easily goes off after other pleasures. Adultery, however, is the rejection of a true and deep love. It is dissatisfaction with God and looks elsewhere for that which only God can legitimately supply. It is only possible when there is no enjoyment of God. Throughout Scripture, God regards himself as bound to his people in the same way as a husband is bound to his wife. Therefore, any sin which causes a Christian to lose his or her love for God is seen as a breaking of the marriage vows. It is spiritual adultery.

Perhaps the most vivid illustration of this is seen in the life of Hosea the prophet. The book of Hosea is remarkable because the prophet's message is lived out in his own domestic life. Hosea is told by God to marry a prostitute (Hosea 1:2). He marries Gomer but then she leaves him and goes back to her lovers and to her prostitution. She sinks so low in the moral cesspool that she is finally sold into slavery. All this time Hosea's love for Gomer does not waver—he even goes to the slave market and buys her back (Hosea 3:2). It is a remarkable story but its spiritual purpose is to show God's love and grace for his people. The picture is that Israel has been like an unfaithful wife to God (Hosea 4:15). Here is an illustration of God and his church in our day.

Gomer has left Hosea—and we as sinners have turned away from God. All efforts to restore and reconcile seem to have failed. There is a threat of judgement (Hosea 2: 4-6) and the withdrawal of divine blessing (vv. 8-9), but then in verse 14 there is a turning point and, from then on, light and hope begin to shine. Divine love works to allure the sinner back to himself.

Hosea 2:14 is the voice of love: 'Therefore I am now going to allure her; I will lead her into the desert and speak tenderly to her.' The allurement of love is stronger than all other forces. All this finds its fulfilment in Jesus. In love, he came to earth to seek and save sinners. The price he paid to set us free from the slavery of sin is a price only divinity could pay. It is no threat of hell that saves the sinner. What allures our souls to God, what finally breaks the resistance of our sin, is the knowledge that God loves us.

Causes

The causes that bring a Christian to such unfaithfulness to God are varied. For some, it is simply that they have a Christianity that is an illusion with no substance, and this is because they were never saved in the first place. Modern evangelistic methods have filled the church with people that are sometimes called 'almost' Christians. The marks of the 'almost' Christian are:

- No commitment or enthusiasm for the work of the gospel. They may be committed to the church and its fabric but not to the spiritual work of the gospel.
- If they know anything at all of private prayer and Bible studies, these are almost certainly a bind or duty and rarely a delight.
- They never face up to the seriousness of their own sin. They rationalize it, excuse it and even justify it, but never repent of it.

The 'almost' Christian faith is like Disneyland—it is pleasant and enjoyable, but really it is nothing more than an illusion.

Sadly, this unfaithfulness is also seen in some Christians who really are saved. Their problem is that their thinking on the Lordship of Christ is all wrong, so there is no authority in their lives and no discipleship. Such Christians cannot understand Paul's command in Ephesians 4:22-24 to put off the old self and put on the new self. Paul's exhortation, 'Put off ... put on,' implies that a conscious effort is needed to change our lifestyle. It is not something that just happens, but is something that has to be worked at. It is no use merely wanting to be a better Christian, or wanting to be more prayerful and more spiritual. One must do something about it. This is not salvation by works—Paul is not dealing here with our

> Perhaps the most common cause of spiritual adultery is that Christians leave their first love.

justification before God, but with the life of one who has already been justified.

Perhaps the most common cause of spiritual adultery is that Christians leave their first love. This is what Jesus accused the Ephesian church of doing (Rev. 2:4). William Still has written of this verse that

> It is not a matter of losing the first emotional experience of conversion, that almost inevitable loss ought to lead to deeper faith, but turning away from the Lord himself, because with carnal zeal we become preoccupied with Christian service. The danger cannot be exaggerated... Not even dutious devotions with quiet times, Bible reading and devout religious observances will take the place of the warm heart and tender love towards the Lord Jesus himself. This must be preserved at all costs.[13]

When love has gone, a measure of faithful habit can continue, but this is only a sham because enjoyment and warmth have gone out of the relationship.

The remedy

There is no remedy offered in Ezekiel 23 but there is in Hosea 10.

The sin of Israel is spelt out clearly in Hosea 10:1-11, but then in verse 12 comes a command from God to break up the unploughed or fallow ground.

In this metaphor, the unploughed ground is afraid of the work God needs to do in it. It is comfortable and does not want to be disturbed. It just lies there, always the same. It enjoys the sunshine of God, but it is hard, barren and fruitless because it is years since the plough has bitten into it. The plough hurts, disturbs, turns over, and digs up things hidden beneath the surface, so it is avoided, as it were, by the ground.

This is a picture of the fallow Christian, and God says, '... it is time to seek the LORD' (v. 12). It is time to break up the fallow ground. There is a need to 'sow for yourself righteousness'. This is not an evangelistic sowing of the Word, but a work needed in the heart of the believer.

When God's Word is sown in our hearts, it produces righteousness—changed lives and deeper commitment. This is how we as Christians are to seek the Lord. It is not an idle waiting for God to do something, but rather a determined effort on our part to draw near to him and to go on doing this 'until he comes and showers righteousness on you'.

FOR FURTHER STUDY

1. Look up the following references: Jer. 3; Ps. 45. Note how the imagery of the Old Testament shows God's love for his people as that of a husband for his wife.

2. Look up the following references: Eph. 5:22,23, Rev. 21:2, and note, similarly, how the imagery of the New Testament shows God's love for his people as that of a husband for his wife.

3. The term 'almost' Christian derives from Paul's preaching to Agrippa (Acts 26:28)— look up this passage in the *Authorized Version*. Can you think of any other people in the New Testament who almost became Christians?

TO THINK ABOUT AND DISCUSS

1. The image of adultery is extremely graphic, and yet it is one which God has chosen to use in showing the violation that sin, especially the sin of idolatry and false worship, brings into his relationship with his church. Mention two or three aspects of worship in the modern church which clearly fall into this category.

2. How may the contemporary church be delivered from its sins of idolatry? What might you be able to do to bring the message of repentance to parts of modern Christendom which you know are caught up in false worship?

11 The watchman

Ezekiel Chapter 33

The fact that Ezekiel was in Babylon ministering to Judah was more than an indication that God had not totally abandoned his people. There was still hope for them!

God told Ezekiel, 'Son of man, I have made you a watchman for the house of Israel; so hear the word I speak and give them a warning from me' (Ezek. 33:7). Behind this appointment of the watchman was the mercy and grace of the Lord: 'As surely as I live, declares the Sovereign LORD, I take no pleasure in the death of the wicked, but rather that they turn from their ways and live. Turn! Turn from your evil ways! Why will you die, O house of Israel?' (Ezek. 33:11).

The sinner's only hope of forgiveness and salvation rests exclusively in the grace of God. Prayer, faith and repentance would be of no use to us if God were not merciful. It was this mercy and grace that was responsible for Ezekiel's presence in Babylon. The God of the Old Testament is as full of grace as the God of the New Testament, and that is because he is the same God. Grace runs throughout all of God's dealings with mankind. It is inaccurate to translate John 1:17, as the *Living Bible* does, 'For Moses gave us only the Law with its rigid demands and merciless justice, while Jesus Christ brought us loving forgiveness as well.' That is paraphrase at its worst. It is not true to the text of John 1:17 and it is not true to the revelation of God in the Old Testament.

> Prayer, faith and repentance would be of no use to us if God were not merciful.

It was not merciless justice that saw God appoint Ezekiel as a watchman in Babylon, but the mercy and grace of a God who longs for sinners to repent.

Warning

The function of the watchman was to give a warning of impending danger (Ezek. 33:1-6). Derek Thomas has written:

> Ancient cities were vulnerable to attack at almost any moment. Consequently, one of the most important civic offices was that of a watchman. Occupying a suitable vantage-point from which he could survey the surrounding countryside, he would blow a trumpet so as to give warning of any approaching parties, whether friendly or not. The amount of time a city would have to get its inhabitants safely within its city walls and ready for defensive action against marauders depended largely on the swift actions of its

watchman. The lives of the people were dependent upon his vigilance... The watchman had a responsibility; to warn of approaching danger. But the people were likewise responsible—to react accordingly. If they failed to run into the city, they had only themselves to blame if they fell under the sword of the invading army.[14]

To be effective, of course, the watchman would need to be able to recognize the enemy. When I was a young man in the Royal Air Force, I was a watchman. Many times in the middle of the night I would be watching the northern approaches to Britain on a radar screen. The threat at that time came from Russia, and it was reckoned that any attack would come from the north. The problem of a radar screen was that every blip looked the same. The radar blips of the American planes did not show the stars and stripes, and the blips of the Russian planes were not red! So, every plane crossing our air space had to submit a flight plan telling what height and speed it would be travelling at certain designated spots. If a blip did not conform to a flight plan, it was considered to be an enemy, and fighter planes were sent up to intercept it.

All Christians are watchmen in the spiritual battle. This battle is not like the old western films, where all the bad characters wore black hats and the good characters appeared in white hats. Everything there was obvious and clear-cut. Our battle is not like that because the devil does not fight that way. In Ephesians 6:11 Paul refers to the devil's 'schemes' or his 'wiles', and we are

> **All Christians are watchmen in the spiritual battle.**

warned of this throughout Scripture. He is crafty (Gen. 3:1) and cunning (2 Cor. 11:3); he will seek to outwit us (2 Cor. 2:11) and set traps (1 Tim. 3:7); he is the father of lies (John 8:44) and can even perform miracles (Matt. 24:24).

You see, then, how careful the Christian has to be. The battle is not always obvious, and sometimes we can lose a skirmish before we are even aware that we are in it. We must therefore be continually on our guard. How often God's people are led into sin through something which seems innocent and harmless! This is due to the wiles and schemes of the devil.

> We must be continually on our guard.

The language the Bible uses to describe our enemy's activities is very expressive. Sometimes he 'prowls around like a roaring lion', and at other times 'masquerades as an angel of light' (1 Peter 5:8; 2 Cor. 11:14). The 'angel of light' is far more dangerous than the 'prowling lion' because, whereas the one will put you on your guard, the other will take you unawares. In the Acts of the Apostles we see the devil as the roaring lion, stirring up his puppets to fierce and bitter persecution of the Christians. He still works like this and will mount direct assaults upon us through various channels. We find the classic example of his coming as an angel of light in Genesis 3, when he approached Eve full of apparent friendliness and concern, and yet craftily cast doubt on the truth of God's Word and character (v. 5).

When the enemy comes as an angel of light, it is the truth of God that exposes him for what he is. No matter how cleverly he masquerades, or how crafty his approach, the devil will always be in conflict with the truth of God as revealed in the Scriptures. God's Word is the searchlight that exposes the wiles of Satan.

Serious

The efficiency of the watchman is crucial not only for the people he has to warn but also for his own well-being (Ezek. 33:5). The world needs Christians who are fearless and reliable in warning it of the consequence of sin.

Men and women without Christ as their Saviour are going to hell. They are not simply going to a 'Christless eternity', as it is often put. They are without Christ now and they are going to exist for ever under the wrath and judgement of a holy God. Christians often ask, 'How can I get a burden for souls?' The answer has to be: read the Bible and believe it; believe what it has to say about the terror of the Lord and the eternity of judgement. Then consider that this is what your unbelieving children and parents and friends will have to face unless they turn to Christ. If that does not give you a burden for souls, then nothing will. If unbelievers are to avoid hell, they must be saved.

> Men and women without Christ as their Saviour are going to hell. They are not simply going to a 'Christless eternity', as it is often put.

Do we care enough for the souls of men and women, or are we indifferent to their salvation? Do we really believe in hell? If one of us had a young child in our family with a terminal illness, we would be terribly grieved. We would feel the matter deeply and be unable to put it out of our minds. This is right and proper; it is a response governed by love and real concern. We would ask our Christian friends to pray for the loved one and plead with God for healing. Physical death is real to us all and we feel its pangs and pain. But somehow eternal death does not seem so real to us. We all have loved ones who are living without Christ and who will go to hell if they die in that condition, yet we rarely shed a tear for their souls. As long as the death of the body seems more important to us than spiritual death, evangelism will always lack the urgency that characterizes New Testament life and witness.

> As long as the death of the body seems more important to us than spiritual death, evangelism will always lack the urgency that characterizes New Testament life and witness.

The early church was a telling church. Why was this? Were not music and drama available as means of communication in the society of their day? Yes, but telling or preaching was God's way of communicating the gospel, and it still is today. The principle presented in Romans 10:14-15 is still relevant: sinners cannot believe unless they hear, and they will not hear unless someone tells them the gospel.

Derek Thomas has spelled out the seriousness of this matter in these words:

We are held accountable for the witness we bear to the lost. Failure to warn a sinner of the consequence of sin renders us 'accountable for his blood' (Ezek. 33:8). Christians can expect to be judged for their failures in evangelism when an opportunity for witness has been given them.[15]

Joy

Why is it that we so often lack enthusiasm for the task of evangelism? The fundamental reason has to be that we have lost sight of the glories of the gospel. We have grown cold, and this is not difficult to demonstrate: it is usually the newly converted who are most effective in telling the gospel and bringing newcomers under its sound. The joy of a new discovery is in their hearts and they feel constrained to share it; theirs is the joy of the woman who has found her lost coin, or the shepherd who has found his lost sheep. Come and 'rejoice with me,' they cry to their friends, their neighbours and to all who will listen (Luke 15:6,10).

These elements of freshness and joy do not have to fade with the passing years, but they will certainly do so if we lose sight of the glories of the gospel. How does this happen? It happens when we lose sight of Christ. Paul wrote, 'God, who said, "Let light shine out of darkness," made his light shine in our hearts to give us the light of the knowledge of the glory of God in the face of Christ' (2 Cor. 4:6). Paul had been a believer for a long time when he penned these words, but the reality of which he wrote still thrilled his soul. Do these and similar words of Scripture also fill you with joy and adoration? After all his experiences, rough and smooth, Paul was still gripped by the love of Christ, moved by his compassion, exultant in his riches. He was still a man in love, not with an idea or theory, but with a person.

Most Christians today find witness difficult and we are always talking about how hard it is to evangelize. There is no doubt that this is true but perhaps we ought to talk more of the joy and privilege of the gospel. This privilege is twofold. First of all, we are believers in Christ and there is no greater privilege. Only when we realize this shall we appreciate the second privilege, that of telling others about the Lord Jesus Christ.

What a joy and privilege it is to speak of these things! And what joy it is to see the Holy Spirit working in the hearts of sinners, to see indifference and apathy turn to concern, concern to conviction, and then conviction to salvation. There is nothing like it! To be a soul-winner makes you feel ten feet tall, but at the same time it makes you feel like dust. It is humbling to realize that God condescends to use a sinner like

> It is humbling to realize that God condescends to use a sinner like you ... to save another soul.

you, with all your faults, to save another soul. Your joy is such that you want to see more souls saved. And there is only one thing that will save sinners: the gospel of Jesus Christ. So you want to tell it with more faithfulness, greater love, greater urgency and greater power. You want success, not just because it makes you feel good, but because God is glorified and sinners are saved from hell.

The watchman or soul-winner is a person with a great longing to see God glorified in the salvation of sinners. The difficulties and problems of witness do not put him off; they serve only to enhance his sense of urgency and drive him to the Lord in earnest prayer.

FOR FURTHER STUDY

1. The Bible emphasizes taking heed to our lives, and to the lives of others. Look up the following references, and note how they apply to you in relationship to yourself and to other people: Acts 20:28; 2 Cor. 13:5.

2. The devil is busy trying to obstruct God's work. Compare the following passages: 1 John 5:19; Eph. 6:10-20.

TO THINK ABOUT AND DISCUSS

1. How could you more effectively be a watchman in the situation in which God has placed you in life?

2. Think of certain areas in which you might be able to share the gospel with people in particular need, such as in retirement homes, in hospitals, among immigrants and refugees, etc. What strategy might you be able to use in taking the gospel to such people?

3. In the light of question 2 above, list in priority the following elements you will want to use:

- Study of the Bible;
- Evangelistic literature;
- Prayer;
- Audio-visual presentation;
- Use of songs, hymns, etc.;
- Testimony;
- Other (please add to the list).

12 Shepherds and sheep

Ezekiel Chapter 34

The great love and concern God has for his people is seen clearly in Ezekiel 34. They are like a flock of sheep who have been neglected by their earthly shepherds, but the heavenly shepherd vows, 'I myself will search for my sheep and look after them' (v. 11).

This love for the sheep reaches its height in verse 23, 'I will place over them one shepherd, my servant David, and he will tend them; he will tend them and be their shepherd.'

Derek Thomas has written:

Having declared that he will be their Shepherd (Ezek. 34:11-16), God now suggests that his servant David will be their shepherd. There is no contradiction, for the passage speaks of the coming of Christ, who is God, of course! ... This passage is a glimpse of the one who called himself the Good Shepherd

(John 10:11), and elsewhere is referred to as the Chief Shepherd (1 Peter 5:4)…This passage is not to be taken as a promise that David himself will return (resurrected) to rule over Israel. Ezekiel is speaking of the return of one like David… It is this idealized David, Jesus Christ, that is in view here.[16]

Amazing love

There is nothing more amazing than the love of God. These sheep were obstinate, stubborn and rebellious (see Ezek.2:3-5) but still God reached out to them. They

> There is nothing more amazing than the love of God

were guilty of great sin but even then there was mercy and forgiveness offered if they would repent. God's love is not soft and weak, as if it cares nothing about sin, but, rather, exactly the opposite. He cares deeply and sin grieves him. While he will not tolerate it or excuse it, he will pardon it, and it is against this backdrop of divine holiness that God's love shines most brightly.

The apostle Paul describes the undeserved nature of God's love for us in the lovely words of Romans 5:6-8: 'You see, at just the right time, when we were still powerless, Christ died for the ungodly. Very rarely will anyone die for a righteous man, though for a good man someone might possibly dare to die. But God demonstrates his own love for us in this: While we were still sinners, Christ died for us.' God shows love to the ungodly. 'Ungodly' means 'unlike God'. Mankind was made in the image of God but sin has so disfigured this image that the whole human race is now ungodly, not loving God or knowing God; the Bible says that people are enemies of God, alien and hostile, at war with God.

The apostle John brings before us this staggering description of divine love: 'This is love: not that we loved God, but that he loved us and sent his Son as an atoning sacrifice for our sins' (1 John 4:10).

Ungodly man does not love God, nor seek to be loved by God. Man's nature and mind are so darkened by sin that he is ignorant of God's love and mercy. He takes the blessings of life for granted: health, food, breath, and the beauty of creation are never acknowledged as gifts of God. We talk about Mother Nature, while the Bible talks about the Creator God. We talk about the Laws of Nature, while the Bible talks about the will and providence of God. Because we exclude God, we do not seek him. *But he seeks us!* In Jesus, God came to seek and save the lost. It was not that we loved him but that he loved us. And what a love! Divine love is not an empty, sentimental pity, but it demonstrates itself in an act of propitiation. Propitiation is the word the *New International Version* translates as *atoning sacrifice* and it means that on the cross, bearing our sin and guilt, Jesus endured the wrath of God instead of us, and paid

> Propitiation: On the cross, bearing our sin and guilt, Jesus endured the wrath of God instead of us, and paid fully on our behalf the debt we owed to God for breaking his holy law.

fully on our behalf the debt we owed to God for breaking his holy law. On the cross our Saviour cried, 'My God, my God, why have you forsaken me?' (Matt. 27:46). The holy God forsook his Son because he was our sin-bearer: 'God made him who had no sin to be sin for us' (2 Cor. 5:21). Jesus was 'stricken by God, smitten by him, and afflicted' (Isa. 53:4). On the cross, the Old Testament prophecy of Zechariah 13:7 was being fulfilled: '"Awake, O sword, against my shepherd," declares the LORD Almighty. "Strike the shepherd..."' The sword was the sword of judgement, and Jesus tells us clearly that this verse speaks of him (Matt. 26:31).

In other words, at Calvary, our Lord made it possible for a holy God to pardon us, even though we were sinners and had broken his holy law. God dealt with the problem of sin in the only way that could satisfy his holy justice and enable him to move in and break the power of Satan in the lives of lost sinners. He did this by punishing the only man that qualified to be our substitute by virtue of his sinlessness, and the only man who, after enduring the wrath of God equivalent to our being in hell for all eternity, could take up his own life again and rise from the grave, that is, a man who was also God himself.

The shepherd

In the Old Testament, the job of being a shepherd was a most menial one. If a man had several sons, it was the youngest that looked after the sheep. David himself was the youngest of Jesse's sons and that was why he was a shepherd. What right did David (or any of us) have to call the holy sovereign God his shepherd? Indeed, is it not rather irreverent to refer to so majestic and awesome a being in this way? The answer to both questions is that the title of Shepherd is one that the Lord had given to himself! David did not invent it, nor did he refer to his Lord as Shepherd because he himself happened to be a shepherd. Even if he had been a fisherman or a shopkeeper, he would have still used this title, shepherd, because from the earliest times in Scripture the Lord had revealed himself to his people in using the picture of a shepherd.

In Genesis 49:24 we read of the dying Jacob speaking to his children and reminding them that their God is the Shepherd, and Rock of Israel. Isaiah, in chapter 40, is likewise reminding Israel who their God is. There is always the tendency to forget the greatness of the Lord, and twice the prophet rebuffs the people: 'Do you not know? Have you not heard?' (vv. 21, 28). He then paints a marvellous picture of our great God as the one who sits upon the circle of the earth, before whom the nations are like a drop in a bucket. In the middle of these thrilling words, the Lord is described as tending his flock like a shepherd (v. 11).

Ezekiel tells us that there are false shepherds who would lead the people of God astray. Nevertheless, the Lord says, 'I myself will search for my sheep and look after them' (Ezek. 34:11). Then he goes on to say, 'I will place over them one shepherd, my servant David, and he will tend them; he will tend them and be their shepherd' (v. 23). The person referred to as David in this verse is not the king who wrote Psalm 23, but David's greater Son, the Lord Jesus Christ. Ezekiel is prophesying of the coming of the Messiah, as, too, is Zechariah, 'Awake, O sword, against my shepherd... strike the shepherd, and the sheep will be scattered' (Zech. 13:7). The day before he died, Jesus quoted this verse and applied it to his death on the cross (Matt. 26:31).

No wonder David delighted in his Shepherd, and the same is true of all believers. All we need, we can find in Jesus. To the troubled heart he can bring peace; to the weary, rest; to the penitent, pardon; and to the weak, strength. Christians lose so much of the joy of salvation by concentrating on what they can do for the Shepherd instead of on what the Shepherd has done and continues to do for them.

The flock is the constant object of his love. He knows every sheep and lamb by name. No human shepherd could be like that—but Jesus has our names engraved on the palms of his hands. There is not a second when his eye wavers from us, not a moment when his prayers and intercession desert us. He sees us all as individuals and loves us with an everlasting love. Therefore, the greatest privilege any human being can have is to know Jesus as his or her Shepherd.

> The greatest privilege any human being can have is to know Jesus as his or her Shepherd.

'The LORD is my Shepherd' is an amazing statement and everything else in Psalm 23 follows on as an inevitable consequence of it. This is not some theoretical proposition and neither is it wishful thinking; it is far more even than just a theological statement. This is the experience of all God's people! This is what we are saved to, and the reality of what we are saved to is known as we submit to the care of the Shepherd. There is no use saying, 'The LORD is my Shepherd,' and then worrying yourself sick about where you are going to find green pastures. If the green pastures and quiet waters are found as a result only of your efforts, you don't need a Shepherd. But the fact is that we all make a terrible mess of life, and we need Jesus to be our Shepherd.

FOR FURTHER STUDY

1. Using a concordance or computer word search, look up as many references as you can find in the Old Testament to sheep and shepherds, and note how frequently this image is applied to believers and their relationship to God.

2. Read the descriptions of Jesus in the following passages: John 10:11; Heb. 13:20. How do these make you feel in your relationship with him?

3. Scripture suggests that not only is Christ the Shepherd, but also a sheep—in fact, a sheep who is offered up as a sacrifice. Look up and compare the following references: Isa. 53:7; 1 Cor. 5:7; Rev. 5:6-9.

TO THINK ABOUT AND DISCUSS

1. How does the fact that God has chosen to be identified in such terms as a humble shepherd make you, as one of his sheep, think you should behave?

2. As you endeavour to be conformed more and more to the likeness of Christ, are there people you can think of who could benefit from any shepherding you could do for them, even simply at the level of helping them to a clearer understanding of the truth, encouraging them to read the Bible more regularly, to attend a Bible-based church, read reliable Christian books, etc.?

13 The valley of dry bones

Ezekiel Chapter 37

The shepherd's care for his flock is demonstrated yet again in chapter 37. Ezekiel's vision of the valley of dry bones is a remarkable story. But the story is only meant, as are all the visions, to convey a truth from God.

This is made clear in verse 11: 'These bones are the whole house of Israel.' Here, God is reminding us that he sees the true spiritual condition of the people and does not minimize it, yet still there is hope in the message that the prophet is to bring to them.

Dry bones

Ezekiel, as the result of the activity of the Holy Spirit (v. 1), found himself in the middle of a valley filled with dead men's bones. They were very dry (v. 2), that is, they had been dead a long time. This was no recent disaster but the product of a long process of decay and death. And the valley was full of these bones—there were very many. It was a total disaster not merely touching one or two people, but the whole nation.

The prophet must have been shocked at what he saw. He had seen nothing like this before, and revulsion must have filled his heart. But the vision was meant by God to do just this; it was meant to hit him hard. God let him take it all in as he led Ezekiel 'to and fro among them' (v. 2). Then God asked his servant a crucial question: 'Can these bones live?' (v. 3). Following the question came the command, 'Prophesy to these bones' (v. 4). Does history, sacred or secular, offer a more ridiculous picture than this? Here is the height of hopelessness! Did any preacher have such a dumb congregation as Ezekiel? Written over the scene in large letters is the word—'IMPOSSIBILITY'.

The valley of dry bones speaks of the spiritual condition of the nation. And if we are to learn anything from this, we have to see that it also speaks of our nation. Do we see our people as God does? Can we see the true spiritual condition of Britain or America, or whatever our nation is, as spiritually dead? God caused the prophet to pass back and forth among bones—and we do this every day in the shops and on the streets of our towns and cities. Do we see? Do we feel the situation? Jesus did, and he wept over Jerusalem. Paul did, and his heart's desire and prayer for his nation was that they should be saved. Consider how John Elias saw his homeland of Wales in 1841:

> The valley of dry bones speaks of the spiritual condition of the nation.

They walk in darkness, without knowing whither they go; and the ministry leaves them in that condition. Oh how sad! God, no doubt, is hiding himself! There is strength, light, and warmth wherever his gracious presence is found. Oh! that he would return to us, for his name's sake! Oh! that he would turn to revive us! We have deserved this on account of our great iniquities, but he can visit us in his grace. Oh! that I might see one gracious and powerful divine visitation, in Anglesey, before I sleep in death.[17]

Obedience

No faith is needed to do the possible. Again and again, God asks people not to do what they can, but what they can't.

> God asks people not to do what they can, but what they can't.

God's dealing with us is not intended to show us how clever we are if only we would try, but rather the opposite, that no matter how hard we try, in the realm of the Spirit, we are helpless. We need to learn to trust God and realize that we can do all things—but only through Christ.

Ezekiel was in a position not of his own choosing. He had been led by the Spirit and not to green pastures but to a valley of death. He must have shuddered at the appalling sight of mile after mile of dry bones. Many in his position would have run away in despair, but not this man. His eyes were on God and his ears were open to the voice of God, so he prophesied, as he was commanded (v. 7).

If the world had viewed this amazing scene, it would probably have certified Ezekiel as insane and locked him away. If many religious people had seen it, they may well have accused the prophet of cheapening the gospel and bringing the church into disrepute. But this man was willing to become a fool for Christ's sake. He did as he was told by God. He said to the dry bones, bones which had no ears, 'Hear the word of the LORD.' I wonder what we would have done? Or, more particularly, what we do now when we are facing souls that are spiritually dead?

like Paul

Very often, to save face, we modify God's commands. We may reason and rationalize, but, in reality, our situation is so desperate that it calls for nothing less than full obedience. We are always the losers by such actions and fail then to see what Ezekiel saw. He saw God working and he saw the impossible happening.

God's question

Before God began to work, he asked Ezekiel a very important question: 'Can these bones live?' The purpose of the question was to ascertain the prophet's reaction to the situation and to see whether he had faith in God. If anyone else had asked the question, there could be little doubt that Ezekiel would have answered that the situation was hopeless. But it was God who was asking, so his answer was—'O Sovereign LORD, you alone know' (Ezek. 37:3).

This man believed not only in a doctrine of divine sovereignty that was theoretical, but in a Sovereign God for whom nothing was actually impossible. The doctrine of

God's sovereignty should be a sweet and blessed comfort in a hopeless and terrible situation. Because of this, the prophet was not unduly pessimistic but neither was he unduly optimistic. He did not say, as he looked at the valley of dry bones, 'We are going to see a great harvest of souls.' In other words, he did not speak in the normal evangelical jargon used on the eve of a campaign. All he said was, 'LORD, you alone know.' He was, in effect, saying that if it can be done, and if it is to be done, then God must do it.

Notice that divine sovereignty is linked immediately to divine omniscience: 'You alone know.' God knows because God ordains and plans. And sometimes, to encourage his people, he reveals in advance to them what he is going to do. He did so for Ezekiel in chapter 36:25-28. The preacher and hymn-writer, Augustus Toplady, used to talk about his Saturday assurances, when, on occasions, God would show him on Saturday how he was going to bless his preaching on the Sunday. This is thrilling. It may be rare but it does happen.

Did Ezekiel reason in this way? God does not play with us. If he is showing me this terrible vision and causing me to feel as well as see the situation, it has to be for a purpose. So with trepidation, humility and a little confusion, but also with faith in God, he said—'LORD, you alone know.'

It may be that the Lord is asking us a similar question today. The spiritual condition of our land is frightening, but is it past hope? Can these bones live today? Can our unbelieving relatives be saved? Can that foul-mouthed, blaspheming man at work come to Christ? Can those pleasant but spiritually lost neighbours who have no time for God be converted? Are we beginning, at last, to have a real concern and burden for lost souls? If so, is that not God's doing, and isn't it a ground for optimism rather than pessimism?

Is God telling us to witness to dry bones such as these, to tell them the gospel? And can we respond, as Ezekiel did, 'So I prophesied as I was commanded'? (v. 7). It may be that we feel totally inadequate to meet the needs of today, but we could not be more inadequate than Ezekiel in the valley of dry bones. Our adequacy is no more the issue than the condition of the bones. What really matters is this: do we trust God to work?

> Are we beginning, at last, to have a real concern and burden for lost souls?

For further study ▶

FOR FURTHER STUDY

1. The Bible's teaching on human inability is not always popularly embraced by Christians today. Look up the following references and see how clear its teaching on this subject is: John 6:44, 65; Eph. 2:1, 4-5.

2. There is a clear and vital connection between the message of the Bible being preached and people coming to faith in Christ as a result. Consider the following passages: Rom. 10:13-15; James 1:18; 1 Peter 1:23-25.

TO THINK ABOUT AND DISCUSS

1. The vision of the valley of dry bones is surely one of the most graphic in all of the Bible. It tells us that as sinners, we are nothing more than dead, lifeless bones, and in need of the triumphant power of grace as the Word of God is preached. This may not be a popular view today, yet it accords with such Scripture passages as those in Question 1 above. When people turn away from preaching, what do they substitute it with? Make a list of the alternatives, and show why they can never substitute the means of grace, preaching, which God has appointed.

2. You may be part of a church or a Christian fellowship where the emphasis on preaching is subtly or blatantly being downplayed. How could you use your influence to help bring a more biblical emphasis to the ministry of the Scriptures?

3. How could you encourage a minister or missionary, one who may be being pressurized into engaging in less preaching and having more alternative activities, to be faithful to his God-given calling to 'preach the Word' (2 Tim. 4:2)?

14 Hear the Word of the Lord

Ezekiel Chapter 37 (continued)

God does not see as we see. Our sin and prejudices blur our view of people, situations and circumstances. And so often we see what we want to see. However, God has no such problems; he sees what is, and if we are to be of any use to God, we must begin to see as he does.

As we look at our nation today, we see millions of people rushing around, working, eating, playing and living. But as God looks, he sees a land full of dry bones; he sees men and women dead in sin. Their bodies may be alive, but spiritually they are dead. Do we see our nation like that? If not, there will not be any sense of urgency in our evangelism.

No matter where you go in the Bible, you will find the same teaching. In the beginning in Genesis 3, God warned Adam and Eve that if they ate the forbidden fruit, they would die. They ate it, but after that first sin their bodies were still alive. They would have noticed no physical difference, and yet there was a terrible difference—they were now dead to God, cut off from him. They no longer wanted God, they no longer loved God, and now they hid from him. They were spiritually dead, and physical death would follow in God's time. From the moment they sinned, they were dry bones.

Adam disregarded God's rule and the result was disastrous. Sometimes we can break man's rules and get away with it—for instance, the speed limits on our roads. But no one gets away with breaking God's rules. Our sin will always catch up with us to accuse us, confront us and condemn us. Sometimes we can break man's rules and good will even come from it. There is a plaque on the wall at Rugby School which commemorates the day when William Webb Ellis 'with a fine disregard for the rules picked up the ball and ran with it'. That particular violation of the rules led to the great game of rugby football! But no good can ever come from breaking God's rules.

Sin brings death—dry bones. Jesus called the Pharisees of his day 'whitewashed tombs' (Matt. 23:27). On the outside they were clean and sparkling but inside full of dead men's bones. That is how God saw them. If this is true, then do we see the implication? If a man is spiritually dead, he cannot make a spiritual response to the gospel. In order to please God, he must first of all have spiritual life—he must be born again. This basic biblical truth shatters the myth of salvation by our own efforts. No matter what a man does in terms of morality, religious observance or kind deeds, it will not save him. In terms of salvation, these things are as valuable as a pile of filthy rags. The teaching of salvation by works—no matter what the works—denies the basic Bible teaching that men and women are dead in sin. We are all like this valley of dry bones.

God's answer

God did not send a social reformer to this valley, neither did he send a politician or an educator; rather, he sent a preacher. Ezekiel was in that valley not at the invitation of the dry bones and not by his own inclination but he was there by the sovereign will of God (Ezek. 37:1). God's concern was to change a terrible situation in that valley. He wanted to bring life to those dead bones, but first he had to deal with Ezekiel. The prophet himself was not a dry bone; he had spiritual life, but he needed to see what God saw, and he needed to feel the burden of it. So it was necessary that he be willing to be God's mouthpiece and bring to the dry bones the one thing essential for them: the Word of God. This is always God's way.

> God did not send a social reformer to this valley, neither did he send a politician or an educator; rather, he sent a preacher.

The only hope for our nations is the sovereign power and love of God, but this does not mean that we have nothing to do. There is the same command for us as there was for Ezekiel. He was to prophesy to those dry bones, and we are to go to men and women around us and we are to preach the gospel. Merely to see the situation and to lament about how terrible it is, and even to acknowledge that our only hope is God, is not enough! God's answer is for the dry bones to hear his Word. What we are to preach to them is not left to our imagination—we are to tell sinners the gospel. Ezekiel's message was spelt out for him, 'This is what the Sovereign LORD says to these bones; I will make breath enter you, and you will come to life. I will attach tendons to you and make flesh come upon you and cover you with skin; I will put breath in you, and you will come to life. Then you will know that I am the LORD' (Ezek. 37:5-6).

There are several things to note about this message. It speaks of what God is going to do. The message of the Bible is always that salvation is God's work. In our days, we are to speak of what God has done in and through the Lord Jesus Christ. Evangelism has to be Christ-centred. Our nation needs to hear about Jesus because people are grossly ignorant of the way of salvation. The gospel offers life in place of death but the fact of spiritual death must be made clear. What use is it to offer life to a man who believes he already has it?

> The gospel is not a hit-or-miss affair, but the sovereign will of God being revealed and accomplished.

So the twin thrust of Ezekiel's message (and of our message) is to be people's sin and its consequence of spiritual death, and God's love in giving us eternal life. In other words, it is law and grace. It is this message alone that gives confidence both to the preacher and the hearer. What confidence Ezekiel must have felt in hearing the 'I wills' of verses 5-6. This, most assuredly, is what God was going to do. The gospel is not a hit-or-miss affair, but the sovereign will of God being revealed and accomplished.

Hearing the Word

As the Word of God was preached, things began to happen. The lifeless, hopeless, impossible congregation began to stir (v. 7). This was not the result of eloquent preaching or force of argument, but clearly the power of God was at work. How can the dead hear? Physically they cannot, but spiritually they will hear when God speaks. The face of spiritual death begins gradually to change, until, under the preaching, the dry bones take on a resemblance of life, though there was as yet no breath in them (v. 8).

Dead souls hear the gospel, and under its message there is a stirring, an awakening. There is a measure of change but there is no life. There is a difference between awakening and conversion, and the preacher is not to be satisfied with the resemblance of life. It is possible to appreciate the gospel, enjoy it, support it, and still be spiritually dead. What is needed is the breath of heaven (Ezek. 37:9-10)—the regenerating power of the Holy Spirit. When this comes, we read 'and breath entered them; they came to life' (v. 10).

> It is possible to appreciate the gospel, enjoy it, support it, and still be spiritually dead.

Awakened or saved?

During the first twenty years of our married life, my wife and I lived in four different houses. They were nice enough places, but not one had much of a garden. So it was a real joy to move into our fifth house, which not only had a nice garden, but also three mature apple trees. The first autumn saw a magnificent crop of apples, and we were determined to save as many as possible. So, after they were picked, we wrapped each one separately in newspaper and stacked them all on wooden trays in the garage. We looked forward with anticipation to having apples all the winter. But by Christmas they were all rotten!

I spoke to a farmer friend about this and he told me that it was because I had picked them too soon. I protested that they had looked ripe. 'Yes,' he answered, 'but did they come easily?' He then explained that the right time to pick apples is when they come away from the branch easily into your hand. 'If you have to tug, leave them,' he said. 'They are not ready for picking and will go rotten.'

That was good advice on picking apples, but it is also good advice on dealing with the souls of men and women. How often in our churches have we been overjoyed to see people make a profession of faith, but within a short time it is obvious that they are not saved, and soon they stop attending church. This is so dishonouring to God. Also, it is a cause of deep disappointment and frustration for Christians, and it often makes those who made the profession extremely hardened against the gospel. They say, 'I was saved and it does not work.'

It is a very real problem. The modern 'invitation system'

> How often in our churches have we been overjoyed to see people make a profession of faith, but within a short time it is obvious that they are not saved ...

aggravates it, but even in churches which do not use this system and where more care is taken in dealing with souls, it still happens. Why is this so? Often, as in my experience with the apples, the cause is ignorance coupled with enthusiasm. We are so eager to see souls saved that we ignore basic biblical principles. As a consequence of this, we hurry souls to a decision before they are ready. How can we know when the right time has arrived to pick spiritual fruit?

Firstly, we must always remember that a true conversion is not the result of human decision, but the work of the Holy Spirit. There are evidences of this divine work. We read in Acts 11:23 that at Antioch, Barnabas saw the evidence of the grace of God. The prime evidence is always conviction of sin, which will lead to repentance. There can be no salvation without this. Conviction will vary in degree from one person to another, but it must be there.

> We are so eager to see souls saved that we ignore basic biblical principles.

In past generations, Christians used to make a distinction between a soul awakened and a soul saved. By 'awakened' they meant that the Holy Spirit was beginning to deal with the person. Conviction was coming and a longing for pardon was being created. But this was not yet conversion. Perhaps today we ought again to make this distinction and not try to hasten the work which the Holy Spirit is beginning.

This does not mean that we should sit back and do nothing. If you see souls that God is awakening, then pray for them. Help and advise them as you are able, but let the Holy

Spirit do his own peculiar work. When, like the apples, they are ripe, they will come easily and no pressure will be needed. There are no rotten apples in a harvest that is reaped by the Holy Spirit of God.

Spiritual life produces its own dynamic. The bones stood up to show that there was now a difference. They were a vast army and invincible under the command of God. The impossible had happened! What an encouragement this is for us today. Can our godless nation be changed? Yes, it can! Only God can do it, but we, like Ezekiel, have the responsibility to see the true situation, to feel it and then to tell the dry bones the Word of the Lord.

FOR FURTHER STUDY

1. As unpopular as preaching may be today, note the emphasis that Scripture itself places on it as the means of grace by which God brings sinners to himself: Acts 20:20, 21, 27; 2 Tim. 4:2-5.

2. The Bible distinguishes between those who are what may be called 'awakened' (i.e., to the fact that they are sinners in need of salvation) and those who are truly converted and who show all the marks of being in a right relationship with God. Look up the following references: Acts 8:18-23; Heb. 6:4-6.

TO THINK ABOUT AND DISCUSS

1. It may be tempting, for the sake of evangelistic statistics, to try to gain converts in an inappropriate way. Mention as many examples as you can of such inappropriate ways.

2. Simply to invite people to 'come to the front of the church building' or to 'raise their hands' has sometimes been seen as one and the same as inviting them to come to the Lord Jesus Christ for salvation. Does a person have to make a physical movement such as this in order to come to Christ? How could a more biblical approach to evangelism be adopted?

3. What specific steps could you take to avoid the 'rotten apple' syndrome used as an illustration in this chapter?

End notes

Chapter 1

1 Sproul and Wolgemuth, *What's in the Bible,* Word Publishing, 2000, p132

2 Sproul and Wolgemuth *What's in the Bible,* p137

Chapter 2

3 Matthew Henry, *PC Students Bible,* 1992/98

4 Matthew Henry, *PC Students Bible*

Chapter 3

5 Sproul and Wolgemuth, *What's in the Bible,* p 137

6 A.W. Tozer, *The Knowledge of the Holy,* James Clark, 1965, p11

7 Dennis Lane, *The Cloud and the Silver Lining,* Evangelical Press, 1985 p24

Chapter 4

8 Matthew Henry *PC Students Bible*

9 Matthew Henry *PC Students Bible*

Chapter 8

10 Derek Thomas, *God Strengthens,* Evangelical Press, 1993, p126-7

Chapter 9

11 Dennis Lane, *The cloud and the silver lining,* p99

Chapter 10

12 Matthew Henry *PC Students Bible*

13 William Still, *And I Saw,* Didasko Press, p19-20

Chapter 11

14 Derek Thomas, *God Strengthens,* p222

15 Derek Thomas, *God Strengthens,* p213, 214

Chapter 12

16 Derek Thomas, *God Strengthens,* p222

Chapter 13

17 Edward Morgan, *John Elias,* Banner of Truth, 1973, p138

OPENING UP SERIES

This fine new series is aimed at the 'average person in the church' and combines brevity, accuracy and readability with an attractive page layout. Thought-provoking questions make the books ideal for both personal or small group use.

Opening up Philippians

ROGER ELLSWORTH

96 PAGES £4.00
1 903087 64 3

In this practical and easy-to-read guide, readers are helped to open up the letter to the Philippians for themselves.

'Laden with insightful quotes and penetrating practical application, Opening up Philippians is a Bible study tool which belongs on every Christian's bookshelf!'
DR. PHIL ROBERTS, PRESIDENT, MIDWESTERN BAPTIST THEOLOGICAL SEMINARY, KANSAS CITY, MISSOURI'

Opening up 1 Timothy

SIMON ROBINSON

128 PAGES £5.00
1 903087 69 4

1 Timothy is an urgent letter to a Christian in the thick of a crisis and a call to the local church to get on with the job God called it to do—spreading the Good News! Simon Robinson applies this message incisively to modern readers.

Opening up Nahum

BY CLIVE ANDERSON

1 903087 74 0
AVAILABLE EARLY 2005

FURTHER TITLES IN PREPARATION

PLEASE CONTACT US FOR A FREE CATALOGUE email: sales@dayone.co.uk
In the United States: ☎ Toll Free:1-8—morebooks
In Canada: ☎ 519 763 0339   www.dayone.co.uk